Sensitive Is The

CW00495151

SECRETS OF THE SENSITIVE

Don't Be Afraid To Be Highly Sensitive

Travis Hubbard

Table of Contents

Chapter 1: 9 Ways To Know If You Are A Highly Sensitive Person.... 6

Chapter 2: 6 Ways To Master Your Emotions 10

Chapter 3: 6 Concerning Effects of Mood On Your Life 15

Chapter 4: 6 Ways To Get Full Attention From People Around You 19

Chapter 5: *6 Ways To Get People To Like You* 23

Chapter 6: 6 Ways To Attract Your Potential 27

Chapter 7: How To Be A Good Public Speaker 31

Chapter 8: 6 Ways To Attract Anything You Want In Life 34

Chapter 9: *Reach Peak Motivation* 38

Chapter 10: Mastering One Thing At A Time 41

Chapter 11: Stop Thinking and Start Doing 44

Chapter 12: 3 Ways To Calm The Emotional Storm Within You 47

Chapter 13: *How to Hold Yourself Accountable For Everything That You Do* 51

Chapter 14: Dealing with Feelings of Failure 53

Chapter 15: *How to Stop Chasing New Goals All the Time* 56

Chapter 16: 10 Facts About Attraction.. 59

Chapter 17: 6 Ways To Achieve Peak Performance 63

Chapter 18: The Power of Developing Eye Contact with Your Client 67

Chapter 19: How To Start Working Immediately 70

Chapter 20: 6 Ways On How To Make Your Partner Feel Loved 74

Chapter 21: How To Be A Better Presenter 78

Chapter 22: Deal With Your Fears Now 81

Chapter 23: This Is Life.. 85

Chapter 24: Becoming a Leader 88

Chapter 25: 4 Ways to Deal with Feelings of Inferiority When
Comparing to Others.. 91

Chapter 26: Feeling That You Don't Have Enough Time 93

Chapter 27: It's All About Networking 97

Chapter 28: How To Find Motivation 99

Chapter 29: 10 Habits of Warren Buffet 105

Chapter 30: Building Confidence 109

Chapter 31: How To Stick To Your Goals When Life Gets Crazy ... 112

Chapter 32: How To Spend Money Wisely. 116

Chapter 33: 9 Habits To Wake Up Early 119

Chapter 34: Do The Painful Things First 124

Chapter 1:

9 Ways To Know If You Are A Highly Sensitive Person

Being highly sensitive is personality trait that some of us may possess. Some people are born with it and some people are shaped by their life experiences, but whatever the reason is, it's there.

Barring all the articles and videos that you will find out there on this topic, my definition of a highly sensitive person is someone who has heightened emotions and sensitivity to the world around them. He or she is also a person highly driven by feelings and of the heart rather than the mind.

If you feel that you may be a highly sensitive person but aren't sure, we are going to explore today how we can identify the signs and traits of this unique personality. We will also address how you can manage your emotions when people come across too strong for your liking.

Here are 9 Ways To Know if You're A Highly Sensitive Person

1.   You Pick Up On Subtile Emotional Cues

If you're a highly sensitive person, it is most likely that you're in tune with physical cues that regular people won't necessarily pick up on. Whether it is through someone's facial expression, your inner intuition towards an unfamiliar person, or picking up hints that someone is unhappy with you even though they try to hide it very well. Being highly sensitive allows you to have a strong radar and 6th sense on these things. More often than not, you are usually right on the money.

2.   Other People's Tone Is Very Important To You

If someone's tone sets you off easily, you may be a highly sensitive person without realising it. Tonality is very important to you, and you get easily put off when someone doesn't speak to you in quite the right way. Other people might have to be vary careful when communicating with you and that could be a problem in relationships if people don't understand that side of you. Communicate to others that you may be offended without meaning it, but that you will just need some time to get past it if they are unknowingly triggering you in some ways.

3.   You Are Driven By Intense Emotions

Does watching a sad movie make you cry but others around you don't? Or do you feel incredibly over-the-top happy while others around you simply feel like it was just alright? If you are a highly sensitive person, it is most likely that intense emotions are what drives you. You feel the extreme end of the spectrum. You may cry your eyes out in happiness or sadness, and that's perfectly fine. Embrace your feelings and don't change anything about you.

4.   You Tend To Withdraw When Things Get Too Much To Handle

When things get incredibly overwhelming, do you feel a need to just crawl away and hide instead of facing the problem head on? When we are driven my intense emotions, sometimes it can work against us. We may feel bulks of sadness and fear that paralyses us from doing anything. If that is you, considering working through these emotions one step at a time and break down the problem you face into smaller chunks.

5.   You Think Deeply About Things

If you have a tendency to question about life and your existence on this earth, you may be a highly sensitive person. As you are more in tuned with the world and the mind, inevitably philosophy will be something that you will naturally gravitate towards. Entertain these thoughts and express yourself in ways that celebrate your uniqueness.

6.   People And Activities Drain You

If hanging out with large groups drain you more than they energise you, or if people's problems are not something that you can handle, you may be highly sensitive. Absorbing all the energy from others can be a very exhausting experience. If you need to, take a step back and spend time alone to recharge your batteries before putting yourself out there again.

7.   There's No Middle Ground

You either feel incredibly happy or incredibly sad, there's no middle ground when it comes to your emotions. You either feel happy to be around someone or you just simply want to avoid them like the plague, you don't have the patience or tolerance to perform niceties to people you feel ambivalent about.

8. You Always Feel Misunderstood

Being highly sensitive could mean that you always feel that people don't understand you or are actually hearing what you say, even if in actual fact that they are and do. You always feel a need for reassurance and double confirmation that everything is heard loud and clear. Don't fall into the trap of having to over-defend your position on something if someone doesn't seem to see eye to eye on you on certain matters. It usually isn't their fault.

9. You Love Nature More Than People

Being around other humans can be exhausting for you if you absorb and feed off their energy all the time. Sometimes nature is one that actually revitalised and recharges you. You feel at home with the birds and the trees, the tranquility, and the peace that nature brings to you. Take time out of your schedule to visit the beach, parks, and gardens energise you and release all the built up emotions that other humans and dumped on you.

Chapter 2:

6 Ways To Master Your Emotions

As reported by Psychology Today, psychology's answer to the question of "What is emotional mastery?" Has evolved over the last century. Early American psychology embraced the "James-Lange Theory," which held that emotions are strictly the product of physiology (a neurological response to some external stimuli). This view evolved when the "Cannon-Bard Theory" asserted that the brain's thalamus mediates between external stimuli and subjective emotional experience.

The concept of emotional mastery wasn't introduced until the 1960s with the Schachter-Singer experiment, where researchers gave participants a dose of a placebo "vitamin." Participants then watched colleagues complete a set of questionnaires. When the colleagues responded angrily to the questionnaires, the participants felt angry in turn. But when the colleagues responded happily, the participants also felt happy. The study's results implied a connection between peer influence and the felt experience of emotion.

The idea that emotions are influenced by outer as well as inner stimuli was furthered by psychiatrist Allen Beck, who demonstrated that thoughts, peer influence and circumstance shape emotions. Beck's research formed the foundation of modern-day cognitive-behavioral therapy, the gold standard of emotional mastery as it's understood today.

The Role Of Emotional Mastery In Life And Society

Feelings and emotional mastery play a role in our subjective experience and interpersonal relationships.

- **Emotions unify us across cultural lines**. There are six basic emotions that are universal in all cultures: happiness, sadness, fear, anger, surprise and disgust. We all experience these feelings, although there are cultural differences regarding what's an appropriate display of emotion.

- **Emotions govern our sense of well-being**. Since emotions are a product of our experiences and how we perceive those experiences, we can cultivate positive emotions by focusing on them. There are 10 "power emotions" that cultivate emotional mastery by creating a base of positive affect. When we incorporate even small doses of gratitude, passion, love, hunger, curiosity, confidence, flexibility, cheerfulness, vitality and a sense of contribution, we set the stage for feeling good about ourselves.

- **Emotional mastery supports healthy relationships**. When you're able to demonstrate emotions that are appropriate to the situation, you're able to nurture your relationships. When you don't know how to master your emotions, the opposite occurs: You might fly off the handle at minor annoyances or react with anger when sadness is a more appropriate response. Your emotional response affects those around you, which shapes your relationships for better or worse.

Learning how to master your emotions is a skill anyone can build in six straightforward steps.

1. Identify what you're really feeling

The first step in learning how to master your emotions is identifying what your feelings are. To take that step toward emotional mastery, ask yourself:

- What am i really feeling right now?

- Am i really feeling…?

- Is it something else?

2. Acknowledge and appreciate your emotions, knowing they support you

Emotional mastery does not mean shutting down or denying your feelings. Instead, learning how to master your emotions means appreciating them as part of yourself.

- You never want to make your emotions wrong.

- The idea that anything you feel is "wrong" is a great way to destroy honest communication with yourself as well as with others.

3. Get curious about the message this emotion is offering you

Emotional mastery means approaching your feelings with a sense of curiosity. Your feelings will teach you a lot about yourself if you let them. Getting   curious   helps   you:

- Interrupt your current emotional pattern.

- Solve the challenge.

- Prevent the same problem from occurring in the future.

4. Get confident

The quickest and most powerful route to emotional mastery over any feeling is to remember a time when you felt a similar emotion and handled it successfully. Since you managed the emotion in the past, surely you can handle it today.

5. Get certain you can handle this not only today, but in the future as well

To master your emotions, build confidence by rehearsing handling situations where this emotion might come up in the future. See, hear and feel yourself handling the situation. This is the equivalent of lifting emotional weights, so you'll build the "muscle" you need to handle your feelings successfully.

5. Get excited and take action

Now that you've learned how to master your emotions, it's time to get excited about the fact that you can:

- Easily handle this emotion.

- Take some action right away.

- Prove that you've handled it.

Learning emotional mastery is one of the most powerful steps you can take to create a life that's authentic and fulfilling.

Chapter 3:

6 Concerning Effects of Mood On Your Life

By definition, mood is the predominant state of our mind which clouds over all the other emotions and judgements. Our mood represents the surface-level condition of our emotional self.

Mood is very versatile and sensitive. Subtle changes in our surroundings or even changes in our thoughts directly affect mood. And consequently, our mood, being the leader of our mental state, affects us, as a whole—even impacting our life directly.

Take notes of these following points so that you can overpower your mood and take complete control of your life.

Here Are 6 Ways How Changes In Your Mood Can Impact Your Life:

1. Mood On Your Judgement and Decision-Making

Humans are the most rational beings—fitted with the most advanced neural organ, the brain. Scientists say that our brain is capable of making one thousand trillion logical operations per second and yet still, we humans are never surprised to make the stupidest of judgements in real life.

Well, along with such an enormous 'Logical reasoning' capacity, our brains also come with an emotional center and that is where mood comes in to crash all logic. Most of the decisions we make are emotional, not logical. Since our emotions are steered by mood, it is no surprise that we often make irrational decisions out of emotional impulses.

But again, there are also some instances where mood-dictated decisions reap better outcomes compared to a logical decision. That's just life.

2. Mood Affects Your Mental Health

While our mood is a holistic reflection of our mental state caused by various external and internal factors, it is also a fact that our mood can be the outcome of some harboring mental illness. Both high degree of euphoria and depression can be an indication of mood disorder—just on two opposite ends of the spectrum.

There is no specific cause behind it except that it is a culmination of prolonged mood irregularities. And mood irregularities may come from anywhere i.e. worrying, quarrelling, drug abuse, period/puberty, hormonal changes etc. If such mood irregularity persists untreated, it may deteriorate your overall mental health and result in more serious conditions. So, consider monitoring your mood changes often.

3. Correlation Between Mood and Physical Well-Being

We have heard the proverb that goes, "A healthy body is a healthy mind". Basically, our body and mind function together. So, if your body is in a healthy state, your mind will reflect it by functioning properly as well. If on the other hand your body is not in a healthy state, due to lack of proper nutrition, sleep, and exercise, then your mind will become weak as well. Yes, according to research, having a persistent bad mood can lead to chronic stress which gradually creates hormonal imbalance in your body and thus, diseases like diabetes, hypertension, stroke etc. may arise in your body. Negative moods can also make you go age faster than usual. So having a cheerful mood not only keeps you happy but also fuels your body and keeps you young. Aim to keep your body in tip top condition to nourish the mind as well.

4. Effect Of Your Mood On Others

This is obvious, right? You wouldn't smile back at your significant other after you have lost your wallet, spilled hot coffee all over yourself and missed the only bus to your job interview.

Your mood overshadows how you behave with others. The only way to break out of this would be to meditate and achieve control over your emotional volatility—believe that whatever happened, happened for a reason. Your sully mood doesn't warrant being hostile with others. Instead, talk to people who want the best of you. Express your griefs.

5. Mood As A Catalyst In Your Productivity

Tech giants like Google, Apple, Microsoft all have certain 'play areas' for the employees to go and play different games. It is there to remove mental stress of the employees because mood is an essential factor in determining your productivity at work-place. According to experts, people with a negative mood are 10% less productive in their work than those who are in a positive mood. This correlation between mood and productivity is an important thing to be concerned about.

6. Mood Change Your Perspective

Everyone has their own point of view. Perspectives of people vary from individual to individual and similarly, it varies depending on the mood of an individual. On a bad day, even your favorite Starbucks drink would feel tasteless. It doesn't mean that they made a bad drink—it means that you're not in the mood of enjoying its taste. So, how you perceive things and people is greatly affected by your mindset. Pro-tip: Don't throw judgement over someone or something carrying a bad mood. You'll regret it later and think "I totally misread this".

Final Thoughts

Our mood has plenty of implications on our life. Though our mood is an external representation of our overall mental state, it has its effect on very miniscule aspects of our life to large and macroscopic levels. In the long run, our mood alone can be held responsible for what we have done our whole life—the choices we've made. Though it is really difficult to control our mood, we can always try. Meditating may be one of the possible ways to have our mood on the noose. Because no matter what happens, you wouldn't want your whole life to be an outcome of your emotional impulses would you?

Chapter 4:

6 Ways To Get Full Attention
From People Around You

The long-term success of someone's life depends on getting the attention of others. Those others can include your teammates, your boss, your life partner, your clients, etc. But how? A person may ask. You cannot get promoted without getting your boss's attention, and your work cannot get appreciated by your teammates without awareness. To lead a healthy personal life, one may need to give attention to and from one's life partner, and of course, without the attention of your clients, how will your business survive?

Fortunately, there is plenty of research on how a human brain works and how it can focus on something. A lot of people have been researching about gaining people's attention for a long time now.

By some researchers, attention has been considered the "most important currency anybody can give you," although attention does make a person feel loved, it also gains your success. Fame can even come through negative attention, but it comes with hate as its price, whereas true and long-term success comes from positive attention. Here are six ways to get full attention from people around you.

1. Stand In A Central Position

When you are at a social gathering or a party, place yourself in a central position. Try to appear more friendly to new people, invite them over to your group, this way people will like you more. When you speak, they will pay attention—standing in a prominent place where everybody can see and talk to you easily will gain you more alert. Be being friendly to new individuals, and you will feel connected to others. Just be confident the whole time, and try to blend well with others and stand in a prominent place; this way, you will get more attention.

2. Leave Some Mystery!

Do you know what Zeigarnik Effect is? This effect suggests that the human brain tends to remember those things more, which is incomplete, as the question in their brain arises how? Where? And what?

This kind of technique is often used by professionals in business meetings, audience-oriented presentations. However, you can also use it in your daily life. When you introduce yourself to someone, don't just spill everything about yourself right away. Give the tiniest bit of pieces of information about something interesting, don't give the details just yet; wait for someone to ask for the details. And someone will surely ask, and you will get the desired attention.

3. Use Body Language

Most of us know how to communicate verbally, but do you know how to communicate non-verbally? Because non-verbal communication is as important as verbal communication. Maintain positive body language, and if you sit back slouched and give some closed-off vibes, it is less likely that you would catch someone's attention. To see some attention, you need to bring more positivity in your conversation and your body language. Don't cross your arms and legs when talking to someone; face them with an open posture and stand with confidence. Don't avoid eye contact but don't overdo it; try to maintain eye contact with everyone around you for a while. This will show your confidence and also builds a connection with others. Be relaxed confidently. Smiling while talking to someone indicates your friendliness and makes them feel welcome; this way, they feel comfortable and give you their undivided attention, but everybody would avoid talking to you if you look moody.

4. Leave An Impression

It is the subconscious habit of a human being to think more about the people who left a good impression on them, try to engage their senses like touch, hear, or vision. Who doesn't like fashion nowadays? Try to wear something fashionable and decent, the kind of outfit that will likely leave a good impression on others. You can also wear something that has a different color or a twist to it. Speak confidently and in a clear voice. You can also put on a lovely perfume, cologne; try not to go overboard with this as nobody likes too much smell even if it is good.

5. Having A Hype Team

Having a hype team can easily capture a lot of attention; when you are in a not so formal setting, bring along your friends, surely they will be more than happy to excite you up. When you talk about your achievements among other people, it may seem to some that you are simply bragging.

Still, when someone else talks about your accomplishments, it increases the interest of other people in you and gains you some positive attention.

6. Find A Way To Sell Yourself Without Bragging

A hype team is not always an option, but selling yourself without bragging is also something that needs to be done. What you don't need to discuss is;

- Your bank balance
- The expensive things you own
- Your occupation
- Your achievement

Conclusion

Brag through storytelling, and everybody loves an inspiring story. A successful person with a humble background always gains some attention. Attention plays an essential role in our lives, and you need to put a bit of effort into gaining it.

Chapter 5:

6 Ways To Get People To Like You

We are always trying for people to like us. We work on ourselves so that we can impress them. Everyone can not enjoy a single person. There will always be someone who dislikes them. But, that one person does not stop us from being charming and making people like us. In today's generation, good people are difficult to find. We all have our definition of being liked. We all have our type of person to select. That makes it very hard for someone to like someone by just knowing their name. We always judge people quickly, even to understand their nature. That makes it hard to like someone.

People always work their selves to be liked by the majority of people. It gives you a sense of comfort knowing that people are happy with you. You feel at ease when you know that people around you tend to smile by thinking about you. For that, you need to make an excellent first impression on people. Training yourself in such a way that you become everyone's favorite can sure be tiring. But, it always comes with a plus point.

1. Don't Judge

If you want people to like you, then you need to stop judging them. It is not good to consider someone based on rumors or by listening to one side of the story. Don't judge at all. We can never have an idea of what's going on in an individual life. We can not know what they are going through without them telling us. The best we can do is not judge them. Give them time to open up. Let them speak with you without the fear of being judged. Assuming someone is the worst without you them knowing is a horrendous thing to do.

2. Let Go of Your Ego and Arrogance

Make people feel like they can talk to you anytime they want. Arrogance will lead you nowhere. You will only be left alone in the end. So, make friends. Don't be picky about people. Try to get to know everyone with their own stories and theories. Make them feel comfortable around you to willingly come to talk to you and feel at ease after a few words with you. Being egotistic may make people fear you, but it will not make people like you. Be friendly with everyone around you.

3. Show Your Interest In People

When people talk about their lives, let them. Be interested in their lives, so it will make them feel unique around you. Make sure you listen attentively to their rant and remember as much as possible about a person. Even if they talk about something boring, try to make an effort towards them. If they talk about something worth knowledge, appreciate them. Ask them questions about it, or share your part of information with them, if you have any on that subject. Just try to make an effort, and people will like you instantly.

4. Try To Make New Friends

People admire others when they can click with anyone they meet. Making new friends can be a challenge, but it gives you confidence and, of course, new friends. Try to provide an excellent first impression and show them your best traits. Try to be yourself as much as possible, but do not go deep into friendship instantly. Give them time to adapt to your presence. You will notice that they will come to you themselves. That is because they like being around you. They trust you with their time, and you should valve it.

5. Be Positive

Everyone loves people. You give a bright, positive vibe. They tend to go to them, talk to them and listen to them. People who provide positive energy are easy to communicate with, and we can almost instantly become friends. Those are the type of people we can trust and enjoy being around. Positivity plays a critical role in your want to be liked. It may not be easy, but practice makes perfect. You have to give it your all and make everyone happy.

6. Be Physically and Mentally Present For The People Who Need You

People sometimes need support from their most trusted companion. You have to make sure you are there for them whenever they need you. Be their for them physically, and you can comfort someone without even speaking with them. Just hug them or just try to be there for them. It will make them feel peaceful by your presence. Or be there emotionally if they are ready. Try to talk to them. Listen to whatever they have to say, even if it doesn't make sense. And if they need comfort. Try to motivate them with your words.

Conclusion

You need to improve yourself immensely if you want people to like you. Make sure you do the right thing at the right time. Make people trust you and make them believe your words. Even a small gesture can make people like you. Have the courage to change yourself so that people will like you with all their heart's content.

Chapter 6:

6 Ways To Attract Your Potential

Do you sometimes feel like you're wasting your potential? And do you also feel unsure about how you can even reach your full potential? If so, you're like any other ambitious person who wants to make the best of his/her life. Because to me, that's what "reaching your potential" means.

We all have limited time on our hands. Some live longer than others. But you and I both know that it's not about how *long* you live, it's about *what you do* with the time you're alive. It's about leaving everything on the table and making sure you live up to your inner drive. Look, when I talk about reaching your potential, I'm not talking about what other people or society thinks we should do with our lives.

When you chase empty goals and objects, you become restless. Instead, chase your *own* potential and forget about everything external. Become the best person you can be. That's the only honourable aim there is. We identified 6 skills that will help you achieve your full potential. Here they are.

1. Self-Awareness

You must be comfortable with who you are and what you are. Don't try to be something you're not. And don't try to change yourself just because others tell you to. Instead, know who you are. And if you don't know, find out. Read, write, think, talk. That's self-awareness: It only requires you to be aware of your thoughts. And when you're self-aware, you automatically learn more about who you are—which is called self-knowledge. But it all starts with being aware. No awareness? No knowledge.

2. Leadership

First, focus on yourself. Fix your own problems. Become a stable person who you can rely on. When you do that, focus on inspiring others to do the same. The best way to help others is to teach them to rely on themselves. Sick and narcissistic people want to make people dependent on them. Leaders teach others to be independent. How? By setting a good example. There's no better way to lead.

3. Writing

Better writing leads to better thinking. And better thinking leads to better communication. Better communication leads to better results in your career. "What?! I never thought the writing was that important!" When you get good at one thing, it will help you to get better at other things. You see? It was only when I started writing that everything "clicked." When you become a better writer, you can easily express yourself and start making connections. That will improve your career in ways you never imagine.

4. Mindfulness

My definition of mindfulness might be different than yours. To be clear, I'm not talking about meditation, yoga, or Zen Buddhism. I'm talking about being a calm and mindful person. A person who's in control of their thoughts and emotions. A person who's solid as a rock. A person who others can rely on. But achieving that inner peace requires much training. I don't think we can ever fully master this skill. But by practicing control over our thoughts, we can get better. My favourite way to become more mindful is to be present. The more I *stay* in the present moment, the more mindful I am. The aim is never to be lost in thoughts. It's to be here.

5. Productivity

The funny thing about mindfulness is that people assume living in the present removes your drive to achieve your goals. The reverse is true. The more present I am, the more desire I feel to improve my life. And how do you improve your life? You already know it. I don't have to tell you that work is the only way to achieve things. Thinking about achieving your goals will not do anything real for you. Become a person who's productive *every day*. Make use of your time. Don't just waste it on watching tv, hanging out with your friends, gaming, or any other mindless routine activity. Know how to get the most results in the least amount of time. That's the ultimate aim of productivity skills.

6. Excellence

I half-assed many things in my life. "Let's just get it over with," was my motto. I was so impatient that I hardly did anything well. I just put in the minimum effort. Hence, I was never the best at anything. But then I realized that excellence is a skill. Look at Robert Greene who took 6 years to write another book. Or Lebron James who worked out during every off-season of his career. Or Helen Keller who published 5 books, despite being deaf and blind. But this is also true for successes that don't get attention in the media. Look at the top salesperson in any given organization who arrives early and leaves late every day. Or the mother who sacrifices nights out and dinner parties to raise her kid with all of her attention and love. That's called excellence.

Chapter 7:

How To Be A Good Public Speaker

Public speaking is perhaps the most common and greatest fear one can endure. People would instead choose to interact with snakes or clowns than people. Just hearing about the words "public speaking" can make our palms go sweaty. But there are a hundred ways to tackle this anxiety and deliver a good speech.

Everyone undergoes physiological reactions like pounding hearts and trembling hands whenever they think about speaking publicly. Be careful to avoid associating these feelings with the sense that you might make a fool out of yourself or perform poorly. On the contrary, some nerves are good. The sweating that you get from the adrenaline rush makes you more alert, and you're then ready to give your best performance. There's no guarantee that your anxiety will completely vanish when you go to the stage facing hundreds of people, but there are ways to overcome it a little. The best way is to prepare yourself beforehand. Take your time to go over your notes. Practice a lot. Audio record or videotape yourself to see where you are lacking, get an honest friend or critique who will point out your mistakes. And once you've become comfortable with yourself, be confident and go out there!

Knowing what type of audience you're going to deal with is essential. Your audience is your main ally. Knowing and understanding them should be your priority. Engage with them by grabbing their attention. Keep the focus on them. Stay flexible and gauge their reactions. Avoid delivering a canned speech because it will only confuse or lose the attention of even the most devoted listeners.

Good communication is never flawless, and trust me; nobody even expects you to be perfect. Putting in the requisite time to prepare will help you overcome your shaky nerves and deliver a better speech. Maintain eye contact with your audience and keep the focus on yourself and your message. Keep a brief outline with you, and it can serve to jog your memory and keep you on task.

Keep thinking positively throughout your speech. It will make you feel more confident about yourself. Don't give a heads up to your fear, and it'll start a cycle of negative self-talk and self-sabotaging thoughts such as "i will start to stutter while addressing them" or "i might forget these points in nervousness." These thoughts will only lower your confidence and increase the chances of you not achieving what you're truly capable of. Affirmations and visualizations are two significant steps of improving your self-confidence. Visualize being successful in your upcoming speeches and imagine the feeling of getting done with it and leaving a positive impact on others.

Prepare yourself for any interruptions, too, and analyze how well you handle them, like sneezing in the middle of your speaking or being unprepared for a question. Do you feel surprised, hesitant, or annoyed? If you cannot handle these situations better, try to self-analyze yourself and practice managing interruptions smoothly. The next time you will get even better at dealing with stuff like that.

The more you'll get confident in public speaking, the more you will avail yourself of opportunities for success. The more you push yourself to speak in front of others, the better you will become at this. Remember, it's not a piece of cake to indulge in public speaking; the more you'll practice, the more you will excel at it. And even if it takes longer, don't doubt your ability and potential, and always be confident and believe in yourself.

Chapter 8:

6 Ways To Attract Anything You Want In Life

It is common human nature that one wants whatever one desires in life. People work their ways to get what they need or want. This manifestation of wanting to attract things is almost in every person around us. A human should be determined to work towards his goal or dreams through sheer hard work and will. You have to work towards it step by step because no matter what we try or do, we will always have to work for it in the end. So, it is imperative to work towards your goal and accept the fact that you can't achieve it without patience and dedication.

We have to start by improving ourselves day by day. A slight change a day can help us make a more considerable change for the future. We should feel the need to make ourselves better in every aspect. If we stay the way we are, tomorrow, we will be scared of even a minor change. We feel scared to let go of our comfort zone and laziness. That way, either we or our body can adapt to the changes that make you better, that makes you attract better.

1. Start With Yourself First

We all know that every person is responsible for his own life. That is why people try to make everything revolves around them. It's no secret that everyone wants to associate with successful, healthy, and charming people. But, what about ourselves? We should also work on ourselves to become the person others would admire. That is the type of person people love. He can also easily attract positive things to himself. It becomes easier to be content with your desires. We need to get ourselves together and let go of all the things we wouldn't like others doing.

2. Have A Clear Idea of Your Wants

Keeping in mind our goal is an easy way to attract it. Keep reminding yourself of all the pending achievements and all the dreams. It helps you work towards it, and it enables you to attract whatever you want. Make sure that you are aware of your intentions and make them count in your lives. You should always make sure to have a crystal-clear idea of your mindset, so you will automatically work towards it. It's the most basic principle to start attracting things to you.

3. Satisfaction With Your Achievements

It is hard to stop wanting what you once desired with your heart, but you should always be satisfied with anything you are getting. This way, when you attract more, you become happier. So, it is one of the steps to draw things, be thankful. Be thankful for what you are getting and what you haven't. Every action has a reason for itself. It doesn't mean just to let it be. Work for your goals but also acknowledge the ones already achieved by you in life. That way you will always be happy and satisfied.

4. Remove Limitations and Obstacles

We often limit ourselves during work. We have to know that there is no limit to working for what you want when it comes to working for what you want. You remove the obstacles that are climbing their way to your path. It doesn't mean to overdo yourselves, but only to check your capability. That is how much pressure you can handle and how far you can go in one go. If you put your boundaries overwork, you will always do the same amount, thus, never improving further. Push yourself a little more each time you work for the things you want in life.

5. Make Your Actions Count

We all know that visualizing whatever you want makes it easier to get. But we still cannot ignore the fact that it will not reach us unless we do some hard work and action. Our actions speak louder than words, and they speak louder than our thoughts. So, we have to make sure that our actions are built of our brain image. That is the way you could attract the things you want in life. Action is an essential rule for attracting anything you want in life.

6. Be Optimistic About Yourselves

Positivity is an essential factor when it comes to working towards your goals or dreams. When you learn to be optimistic about almost everything, you will notice that everything will make you satisfied. You will attract positive things and people. Negative vibes will leave you disappointed in yourself and everyone around you. So, you will have to practice positivity. It may not be easy at first while everyone around you is pushing you to negativity. That is where your test begins, and you have to prove yourself to them and yourself. And before you know it, you are attracting things you want.

Conclusion

Everyone around us wants to attract what they desire, but you have to start with yourself first. You only have to focus on yourself to achieve what you want. And attracting things will come naturally to you. Make sure you work for your dreams and goals with all your dedication and determination. With these few elements, you will be attracting anything you want.

Chapter 9:

Reach Peak Motivation

Remember the time when you wanted a sign, a person, a comment, an event, just anything that could maybe make you realize once again that everything is happening for real and that you actually have a presence? Remember the feeling?

I am sure we all had those times. And we often still have and maybe have some more to come. But the question is a big mystery that everyone goes through with a rough answer alongside it.

We all have a vague idea somewhere in our heads. We all have some idea somewhere wandering within us but we cease t find it with all our efforts going in vain. There is this struggle with the world that we keep fighting and then there is this quest that we always seem to be on, where we keep looking for answers.

Let me give you some tips for that. You are looking for motivation within yourself because you think the world can't do one for you. It is true to most extent, but the world is not your servant. Nature still gives you things to be proud of and be inspired from. But we keep neglecting the signs of nature.

Situations often present themselves as if we are not meant to be where we are right now. It may be true. But then the world starts to push you down, you will always find reasons at the bottom from where you would want to take a new step forward!

You will always find new ways to become motivated and inspired. Because you need to be dead to become hopeless and motionless, not wanting to do one more thing that could contribute towards a better life.

Till the day you are alive, it's a sin for you to feel hopeless and without purpose.

The fear of failure is always real. But the fear of not being able to feel content and happy once you reach the top is not a reason to not look or stop looking for newer and better things.

Life has endless possibilities and not all have to be bad always. You will get bigger and better chances more than often. But you have to remain motivated enough to avail them for better once they finally present themselves.

You don't have to be bad to fail at something. Even the best of the best fail and they fail more than a regular person. But that doesn't give them a reason to stop rather they get more motivated and energetic to stick to the cause and for what they believe in.

If one thing is important enough and you believe in it enough you will always stay connected to that thing someway or somehow.

But for that, you have to believe in your abilities. That no matter what happens, if you stay committed enough, there is no way in heaven or hell that can keep you away from success and the things that you most want in your life.

Every mountain is within reach if you keep going and keep believing that you are one more step close to the summit.

Chapter 10:

Mastering One Thing At A Time

I don't think anyone needs any explanation for the phrase, "Jack of all trades, Master of none". If you are one of those people who still can't get a grasp of this simple yet effective phenomenon, you seriously need to revisit your approach to life.

No one can be a true master. It's only a title for comparison. Mastering even one thing can be a task that can take decades. And once you become one, you can't guarantee you would remain the only person eligible for the title.

Yes, you would argue that you want to perfect everything because you want a better life and don't want any acknowledgment or applause. And I know it is well justified, but you need to focus on the bigger things.

Acknowledgment is important. It gives us the confidence to do more. But satisfying others for them to satisfy you is a stupid reason to pursue something. There is a lot of big fish out there for you to go and hunt.

You can go running around all day fetching small motives and goals, which would never profit you in the long run of life. Bigger chances always lie around us, but we are always too distracted to wait and get a good grasp of just one.

Instead of holding onto the one major thing, we cling to countless small ones and end up getting a little bit of everything. But we want everything and a lot of it, as our nature dictates us.

But the truth is simple yet harsh, "You can't always get what you want". You will never be able to get a hold of everything. But you can be good at just one thing and then try to make up the ladder with other singular things, goals, desires, wishes. And who knows, they might eventually get granted one by one.

We spend our life chasing so many things that we eventually get to a point where we are so exhausted that nothing encourages us and we end up giving away all the hard work that we put in.

But life isn't always about giving up on everything else just for the sake of one thing. This misconception is common for everyone that if I go for one goal only, I might not get another chance for the others I had dreamt of.

You need to set your priorities straight. If you have a long-term goal, you need to go for the basics first and gradually climb up the ladder for the ultimate ideal for success.

But consistency and dedication are the traits that once you develop will always help you master everything that you ever come across till your last day on this planet.

Learn to say no to everything that gets in between you and your task at hand. Set your goals for the day and execute everything one by one. Don't leave anything half done, rather give every task your whole effort and your every new venture will see the dawn.

Chapter 11:

Stop Thinking and Start Doing

What is going on around you right now? I am not asking this rather telling you because I know most of you are already thinking the same question. You should be asking this question, or should you?

We are a two-faced species. We say something upfront but we adopt the opposite for ourselves at the same time. We want to install a certain methodology in everyone around us but we are ashamed to do the same thing ourselves.

Fear is a more appropriate and less offending word some might say. But why is it? Is something harmful, or something that doesn't make sense only when you yourself are in the same place as others that followed you?

So show off when we don't have something good to contribute in our own lives? Why be a hypocrite who doesn't even have the guts to admit that they are the timidest and lucid person and they want to follow their own instincts?

You have to make those small changes in your life. That will one day result in a bigger change and elevate your life to that ultimate stature, then you are probably dead.

Stop preaching, stop playing around, stop thinking, worrying, wondering, doubting fearing, hoping for some easy way out! Learn to say STOP to everything that goes against your instincts and your wishes for a better tomorrow.

Do you think you are grinding away yourself every day so you deserve a break? No!

What makes you think you have achieved all you can?

Sure you have done a lot in your life, sometimes it was due to circumstances, sometimes your talents, and sometimes just pure luck. But you went through it then and you were very less competent back then! So why can't you do some more things like those, just easier?

You can and you will! Because now you have grown within and have more experience to tackle what needs to be tackled.

If you keep telling yourself and keep thinking, "Oh this wasn't meant to happen", or "Was it my fault?", or "Why does it always have to be me?", you will quite look over your shoulder searching for the easy way out!

Learn to live by the chances that you keep getting every day. Because is too short to be wondering and never to lift a finger and point in the direction of what needs to be done.

Don't act like you are totally blank and have no idea what to do next. Take a moment and your instincts will naturally take you to the best possible solution.

But you have to get up, go out and start pursuing. Because you are your first priority, always was and always should be.

There is a time in everyone's life when they just need to stop thinking and start doing. That time is always the previous second. The day you understand this puzzle, give yourself a tap on the shoulder because you have finally outgrown yourself

Chapter 12:

3 Ways To Calm The Emotional Storm Within You

When emotions are already intense, it's often hard to think about what you can do to help yourself, so the first thing you need to work on is getting re-regulated as quickly as possible. Here are some fast-acting skills that work by changing your body's chemistry; it will be most helpful if you first try these before you're in an emotional situation, so you know how to use them.

1. Do a forward bend

This is my favourite re-regulating skill. Bend over as though you're trying to touch your toes (it doesn't matter if you can actually touch your toes; you can also do this sitting down if you need to, by sticking your head between your knees). Take some slow, deep breaths, and hang out there for a little while (30 to 60 seconds if you can). Doing a forward bend actually activates our parasympathetic nervous system – our 'rest and digest' system – which helps us slow down and feel a little calmer. When you're ready to stand up again, just don't do it too quickly – you don't want to fall over.

2. Focus on your exhale with 'paced breathing'

It might sound like a cliché but breathing truly is one of the best ways to get your emotions to a more manageable level. In particular, focus on making your exhale longer than your inhale – this also activates our parasympathetic nervous system, again helping us feel a little calmer and getting those emotions back to a more manageable level. When you inhale, count in your head to see how long your inhale is; as you exhale, count at the same pace, ensuring your exhale is at least a little bit longer than your inhale. For example, if you get to 4 when you inhale, make sure you exhale to at least 5. For a double whammy, do this breathing while doing your forward bend.

These re-regulating skills will help you to think a little more clearly for a few minutes, but your emotions will start to intensify once more if nothing else has changed in your environment – so the next steps are needed too.

3. Increase awareness of your emotions

In order to manage emotions more effectively in the long run, you need to be more aware of your emotions and of all their components; and you need to learn to name your emotions accurately. This might sound strange – of course you know what you're feeling, right? But how do you know if what you've always called 'anger' is actually anger, and not anxiety? Most of us have never really given our emotions much thought, we just assume that what we think we feel is what we actually feel – just like we assume the colour we've always called 'blue' is actually blue; but how do we really know?

Sensitive people who have grown up in a pervasively invalidating environment often learn to ignore or not trust their emotional experiences, and try to avoid or escape those experiences, which contributes to difficulties naming emotions accurately. Indeed, anyone prone to emotion dysregulation can have trouble figuring out what they're feeling, and so walks around in an emotional 'fog'. When you're feeling 'upset', 'bad' or 'off', are you able to identify what emotion you're actually feeling? If you struggle with this, consider each of the following questions the next time you experience even a mild emotion:

- What was the prompting event or trigger for the feeling? What were you reacting to? (Don't judge whether your response was right or wrong, just be descriptive.)

- What were your thoughts about the situation? How did you interpret what was happening? Did you notice yourself judging, jumping to conclusions, or making assumptions?

- What did you notice in your body? For example, tension or tightness in certain areas? Changes in your breathing, your heart rate, your temperature?

- What was your body doing? Describe your body language, posture and facial expression.

- What urges were you noticing? Did you want to yell or throw things? Was the urge to not make eye contact, to avoid or escape a situation you were in?

- What were your actions? Did you act on any of the urges you noted above? Did you do something else instead?

Going through this exercise will help you increase your ability to name your emotions accurately. Once you've asked yourself the above questions, you could try asking yourself if your emotion fits into one of these four (almost rhyming) categories: mad, sad, glad, and afraid. These are terms I use with clients as a helpful starting point for distinguishing basic emotions, but gradually you can work on getting more specific; emotions lists can also be helpful.

Chapter 13:

How to Hold Yourself Accountable For Everything That You Do

Staying on top of your work can be difficult without a manager over your shoulder. So how exactly do you manage yourself? I don't know about you, but I have a problem. I am ambitious; I am full of great ideas. I am also, however, extremely undisciplined. But the other day, I had an idea. What if I became "my manager"? Not a bad idea.

Contrary to what the multi-million dollar management training industry says, I don't think management is rocket science (though I am not saying it is easy). A good manager motivates and supports people and makes people accountable. To manage ourselves, we simply need to take concrete steps to motivate ourselves and make ourselves accountable.

1. Create a Personal Mission Statement

I think we get so caught up in the mundane details of daily life that we often lose track of why we're here, what we want, and, most importantly, what we value. Manage yourself by finding a way to integrate your values into what you do. Write your mission statement.

My mission statement, at the moment, is this: "To live simply and give selflessly, and to work diligently towards financial independence and the opportunities such independence will afford me."

Your mission statement doesn't have to be profound or poetic – it just needs to convey your core values and define why you do what you do each day. (Hint: If you can't find a mission statement that fits your current career or life, maybe it is time for a change!

2. Set Micro-Goals

There are countless benefits to writing down goals of all sizes. Annual, five-, and ten-year goals can help you expand on your mission statement because you know you are working towards a tangible result. But long-term goals are useless unless you have a strategy to achieve them. Manage yourself by setting micro-goals.

What is a micro-goal? I like to think of it as a single action that, when accomplished, serves as a building block to a much larger goal.

For example, the resolution to make a larger-than minimum monthly payment on a credit card balance is a micro goal. Each month you successfully increase your payment, you are closer to your big goal of getting out of debt.

At work, a micro-goal might involve setting up an important client meeting. Getting all the elements for a meeting in place is one step towards a larger goal of winning or increasing a particular business relationship.

A micro goal is not, however, anything that goes on your to-do list. Responding to a customer inquiry or cleaning out your cubicle is not a micro-goal unless, of course, you have bigger goals to specifically involving that customer or to get more organized.

Chapter 14:

Dealing with Feelings of Failure

Life is full of ups and downs because of which even the strongest person can feel let down. But this doesn't always mean that it's the end. As the famous quote states, "failure is A step closer to success. "Indeed, there are many reasons for feeling hopeless and feeling like you have failed in life, but there is always A way to overcome every type of failure, be it bad grades at school, being let down by friends, or even having problems in relationships. These are some of the many reasons why A person feels like they have failed in life.

The main focus in overcoming this feeling is analyzing the reason for this failure. For example, if A person fails an exam. They should first own this mistake. This is not easy to do, but by doing so, one can become A better person by trying hard next time. There is always A chance of life improvement. Feeling bad is not A bad thing to do as compared to suppressing the feelings. By suppressing the feelings, regrets can build up, which can further lead to bad habits like addiction and self-harm. Staying away from people who live by quotes like "once A failure, always A failure. " These types of people are the reason why others feel like they are no good and have not done enough. If you start believing this, you can never accomplish anything in life.

Developing healthy habits and eating healthy can lead to optimism which in turn leads to accomplishments. Reading motivational books and attending motivational seminars can help you overcome this feeling because they encourage you to try again with your best effort, which is A very good way to achieve success. Even accepting that you have failed is A healthy step because the burden is reduced once you accept your mistakes. Lastly, you need to evaluate what went wrong with the thing that you've failed in. Evaluating your failures gives you an idea about what not to do next time. Failure should not be seen as A threat, and failure is just an opportunity of proving yourself next time. Without failure, there is no chance of betterment.

Failure teaches you many things, and it teaches you that no human being is perfect, and everyone can make A mistake at some point in their lives. People who have not suffered failure are not perfect, they have A very narrow view of the world around them, and they expect perfection in others. They are very difficult to deal with because of their uncompromising nature. A person who has experienced any kind of failure is very accepting when it comes to people who are having A problem with something and are very eager to help them because they can see themselves suffering from failure in the past. This is A very good trait because nowadays, every other person demands perfection.

Failure is never A defeat and should never be seen as A threatening scenario. There is mostly an option to try again, and those who believe in themselves are the ones that come back strong. There is always an option of seeking help from friends or colleagues, so never hesitate to ask. You can always stand taller after falling. The ups and downs in our lives show that we are alive; the single straight line is merely for the dead.

Chapter 15:

How to Stop Chasing New Goals
All the Time

The philosopher Alan Watts always said that life is like a song, and the sole purpose of the song is to dance. He said that when we listen to a song, we don't dance to get to the end of the music. We dance to enjoy it. This isn't always how we live our lives. Instead, we rush through our moments, thinking there's always something better, there's always some goal we need to achieve.

"Existence is meant to be fun. It doesn't go anywhere; it just is." Our lives are not about things and status. Even though we've made ourselves miserable with wanting, we already have everything we need. Life is meant to be lived. If you can't quit your job tomorrow, enjoy where you are. Focus on the best parts of every day. Believe that everything you do has a purpose and a place in the world.

Happiness comes from gratitude. You're alive, you have people to miss when you go to work, and you get to see them smile every day. We all have to do things we don't want to do; we have to survive. When you find yourself working for things that don't matter, like a big house or a fancy car, when you could be living, you've missed the point. You're playing the song, but you're not dancing.

"A song isn't just the ending. It's not just the goal of finishing the song. The song is an experience."

We all think that everything should be amazing when we're at the top, but it's not. Your children have grown older, and you don't remember the little things.

"…tomorrow and plans for tomorrow can have no significance at all unless you are in full contact with the reality of the present since it is in the present and only in the present that you live."

You feel cheated of your time, cheated by time. Now you have to make up for it. You have to live, make the most of what you have left. So you set another goal.

This time you'll build memories and see places, do things you never got the chance to do. The list grows, and you wonder how you'll get it all done and still make your large mortgage payment. You work more hours so you can do all this stuff "someday." You've overwhelmed yourself again.

You're missing the point.

Stop wanting more, <u>be grateful for</u> today. Live in the moment. Cherish your life and the time you have in this world. If it happens, it happens. If it doesn't, then it wasn't meant to; let it go.

"We think if we don't interfere, it won't happen."

There's always an expectation, always something that has to get done. You pushed aside living so that you could live up to an expectation that doesn't exist to anyone but you. The expectation is always there because you gave it power. To live, you've got to let it go.

You save all your money so that you can retire. You live to retire. Then you get old, and you're too tired to live up to the expectation you had of retirement; you never realize your dreams.

At forty, you felt cheated; at eighty, you are cheated. You cheated yourself the whole way through to the end.

"Your purpose was to dance until the end, but you were so focused on the end that you forgot to dance."

Chapter 16:

10 Facts About Attraction

Everything from taking an interest in someone to admire someone physically or mentally is known as an attraction. The attraction could be a romantic or sexual feeling. Attraction can be confusing and takes time to understand. Most of us find it hard to know what we feel about or are attracted to someone. We couldn't figure out what type of attraction it is, but we should remember there is no right way to feel the attraction. There are so many types of attraction, and some could happen at once.

1. Women attracted to older men:

So, it is expected that most women these days are attracted to older men just because of their "daddy issues" and the most one is the financial issue but according to study it's not the reason. According to authentic references or studies, the women born to old fathers are attracted to older men, and the women born to younger men are attracted to younger men. As they think that they will treat them just like their father did.

2. Opposite attraction:

As we all heard before, "opposite attracts." well, it is true, according to a study of the university of dresden, that both men and women are attracted to different leukocyte antigens, which is also known as the hla complex. A genetic blueprint responsible for the immune function is so unique that this attraction has to do with species' survival. Now, how do our brains detect the opposite hla complex? According to a study, our brain can see the opposite hla complex only by the scents; isn't it a fascinating fact?

3. The tone of women's voices:

According to a study by the university of canada, when women flirt, their voice pitch increases automatically. Not only while flirting, but women's voice tones increase at different emotions. The highest tone of a woman's voice gets when she is fertile or ovulated, and guess what? According to studies, men like the most high-pitched voices of women.

4. Whisper in the left ear:

According to a study, when you want to intimate someone, like whispering " i love you" in their ear, then whisper in their left ear because whispering in the left ear has 6% more effect than a whisper in the right one.

5. Red dress:

Red dress attracts both men and women. It is examined in a study that usually men love women in the red dress. They find it intimidating.

6. Men with beard:

Women find men attractive with a beard. Beard with the subtle cut. Another fantastic fact about the beard is that women judged men with a beard to be a better choice for a long-term relationship. This might be because men with beards look more mature and responsible. Beard also makes you look like you have a higher status in society.

7. Men trying to sound sexy:

So, women have no trouble whatsoever changing their voice, but men have no clue about it. Women lower their voice pitch and make it sexy, and men find it so attractive, but men find it very difficult to sound sexy. It got a little bit worse when men tried to say sexy. The reason behind this is elaborated in research, according to which men are not focused on making their voice sexy but women do.

8. Competing:

Research shows that when you are famous for everyone, and everyone likes them, you get attracted to them and try to get them. You start competing for that person with other people, which makes you feel more attracted to that person. That person will be in your head all the time because you see everyone admiring and chasing that person.

9. Adrenaline:

Studies show that adrenaline has to do a lot with attraction. People find others more attractive when they are on an adrenaline rush themselves. According to a study, women find men more attractive when they are ovulating than in another period.

10. Weights and heights:

When taking a liking to someone. People always prefer to choose a person who holds the right weight and height according to them. Different people may have different opinions. When they find a person with a likable body, they get easily attracted to them.

Conclusion:

Attraction to someone can play a significant role in getting them. When people are attracted to you, they make you feel worth it all, and you feel ecstatic. Attraction can be=ring in a lot of factors like popularity, relationship and of course, love.

Chapter 17:

6 Ways To Achieve Peak Performance

To be successful requires much more than just your intelligence and talent. There are basic needs which have to be met to function at your peak. These basic needs are neglected by most, impairing their capacity to rise to those elusive higher levels of success and happiness in life.

1. Get enough sleep

Sleep deprivation means peak performance deprivation. Without proper sleep you wake up to meet the day feeling scatterbrained, foggy and unfocused. You grab your cup of coffee to get a charge on your brain, which completely depletes your brain function over the course of the day, making your brain even more exhausted.

Good sleep improves your ability to be patient, retain information, think clearly, make good decisions and be present and alert in all your daily interactions. Sleep is your time off from problem solving.

When you get the proper rest your brain becomes awake, alive and ready to generate the cognitive prowess and emotional regulation you need to function at your peak performance.

2. Drink lemon water

Lemon water is a great substitute for your morning coffee. Although lemons do not contain caffeine, lemon water has excellent pick-me-up properties without negative side effects. It energizes the brain, especially if it is warm, and hydrates your lymph system.

Among the most important benefits of lemon water are its strong antibacterial, antiviral, and immune-boosting power, making sick days from work nearly non-existent. Lemon water cures headache, freshens breath, cleanses the skin, improves digestion, eliminates PMS with its diuretic properties and reduces the acidity in the body.

Most importantly, lemon water increases your cognitive capacity and improves mood with its stimulating properties on the brain, helping you to operate more consistently in your peak performance zone.

3. Get daily exercise

Exercise is the best way to reduce the stress that impairs your performance stamina. Exercise increases your "happy" mood chemicals through the release of endorphins. Endorphins help rid your mind and body of tension alleviating anxiety helping you to calm down.

The brain needs physical activity to stay flexible. Exercise stimulates neurogenesis, or the growth of new brain cells, which improves overall brain function. The development of new brain cells keeps your brain young and in shape, allowing you to be more efficient, pliable and clear in your decision making, higher thinking and learning capacities. Neurogenesis is the catalyst to peak performance.

Further, there is nothing that can bring down self-esteem quicker than not liking how you look. Exercise improves self-confidence and your perception of your attractiveness and self-worth. This confidence contributes greatly to your success, prompting people to respect you and take you seriously

4. Have emotional support

Having healthy, loving relationships increases your happiness, success and longevity by promoting your capacity to function in life as your best self. Social connectedness and love gives you relationships to be motivated for and people to be inspired by.

A strong social network decreases stress, provides you with a sense of belonging and gives your life the deeper meaning it needs. When you are loved and loving, and carving out quality time to cultivate these relationships, you are exalted, elevated and encouraged to live your dreams fully.

5. Be unapologetically optimistic

A requirement of peak performance is to look for the best in every situation. Optimism is the commitment to believe, expect and trust that things in life are rigged in your favor. Even when something bad happens, you find the silver lining.

A positive outlook on life strengthens your immune system and the emotional quality of your life experiences, allowing you to be resilient in the face of fear, stress and challenge.

Being an optimist or a pessimist boils down to the way you talk to yourself. When you are optimistic you are fierce in the belief it is your own actions which result in positive things happening. You live by positive affirmation, take responsibility for your own happiness and anticipate more good things will happen for you in the future.

When bad things happen you do not blame yourself, you are simply willing to change yourself.

6. Have time alone

Time alone is refueling to your physical, mental, emotional and spiritual self. This time recharges you, helping to cultivate your peak performance levels again and again. You must give yourself time to recover from the stress of consistently being around others. Being around people continuously wears down your ability to regulate your emotional state, causing self-regulation fatigue. For this reason you must give yourself permission to take the pressure off and disconnect.

Chapter 18:

<u>The Power of Developing Eye Contact with Your Client</u>

We've all heard the age-old saying the "eyes are the window to the soul," and in many ways, it holds. Everybody knows looking others in the eyes is beneficial in communication, but how important is eye contact, and how is it defined?

Eye contact can be subtle or even obvious. It can be a glaring scowl when a person is upset or a long glance when we see something off about someone else's appearance. It can even be a direct look when we are trying to express a crucial idea.

1) Respect

In Western countries like the United States, eye contact is critical to show and earn respect. From talking to your boss on the job or thanking your mom for dinner, eye contact shows the other person that you feel equal in importance.

There are other ways to show respect, but our eyes reflect our sincerity, warmth, and honesty.

This is why giving and receiving eye contact while talking is a surefire sign of a good conversation. Nowadays, it's common for people to glance at their phones no matter if they're in the middle of a conversation or not. That's why eye contact will set you apart and truly show that you give them your full and undivided attention.

2) Understanding

Sometimes locking glances is the only sign you need to show someone that you understand what they are talking about. More specifically, if you need to get a vital point across, eye contact is the best way to communicate that importance. Eye contact is also a form of background acknowledgment like saying "yeah" and "mhmm."

That means it shows the speaker that you are tuned in to and understand what they are saying.

3) Bonding

When someone is feeling an emotion or just performing a task, the same neurons that shine in their brain light up in someone else's brain who is watching them. This is because we have "mirror neurons" in our brains that are very sensitive to facial expressions and, most importantly, eye contact.

Direct eye contact is so powerful that it increases empathy and links together emotional states. Never underestimate the power of eye contact in creating long-lasting bonds.

4) Reveal Thoughts and Feelings

We have countless ways of describing eyes, including "shifty-eyed," "kind-eyed," "bright-eyed," "glazed over," and more. It's no wonder just about every classic love story starts with "two pairs of eyes meeting across the room." Eye contact is also a powerful form of simultaneous communication, meaning you don't have to take turns doing the communicating.

Ever wonder why poker players often wear sunglasses inside? It's because "the eyes don't lie." We instinctually look into people's eyes from birth to try and understand what they are thinking, and we continue to do it for life.

Chapter 19:
How To Start Working
Immediately

"There is only one way for me to motivate myself to work hard: I don't think about it as hard work. I think about it as part of making myself into who I want to be. Once I've chosen to do something, I try not to think so much about how difficult or frustrating or impossible that might be; I just think about how good it must feel to be that or how proud I might be to have done that. Make hard look easy." - Marie Stein.

Motivation is somewhat elusive. Some days you feel it naturally, other days you don't, no matter how hard you try. You stare at your laptop screen or your essay at the desk, willing yourself to type or write; instead, you find yourself simply going through the motions, not caring about the work that you're producing. You're totally uninspired, and you don't know how to make yourself feel otherwise. You find yourself being dissatisfied, discouraged, frustrated, or disappointed to get your hands on those long-awaited tasks. While hoping for things to change and make our lives better overnight magically, we waste so much of our precious time. Sorry to burst your bubble, but things just don't happen like that. You have to push yourself off that couch, turn off the phone, switch off Netflix and make it happen. There's no need to seek anyone's permission or blessings to start your work.

The world doesn't care about how tired you are. Or, if you're feeling depressed or anxious, stop feeling sorry for yourself while you're at it. It doesn't matter one bit. We all face obstacles and challenges and struggles throughout our days, but how we deal with those obstacles and difficulties defines us and our successes in life. As James Clear once said, "Professionals stick to the schedule, amateurs let life get in the way. Professionals know what is important to them and work towards it with purpose; amateurs get pulled off course by the urgencies of life."

Take a deep breath. Brew in your favorite coffee. Eat something healthy. Take a shower, take a walk, talk to someone who lifts your energy, turn off your socials, and when you're done with all of them, set your mind straight and start working immediately. Think about the knowledge, the skill, the experience that you'll gain from working. Procrastination might feel good but imagine how amazing it will feel when you'll finally get your tasks, your work done. Don't leave anything for tomorrow. Start doing it today. We don't know what tomorrow might bring for us. If we will be able even to wake up and breathe. We don't know it for sure. So, start hustling today. You just need that activation energy to start your chain of events.

Start scheduling your work on your calendar and actually follow it. We may feel like we have plenty of time to get things done. Hence, we tend to ignore our work and take it easy. But to tell you the truth, time flickers by in seconds. Before you know it, you're already a week behind your deadline, and you still haven't started working yet. Keep reminding yourself as to why you need to do this work done. Define your goals and get them into action. Create a clear and compelling vision of your work. You only achieve what you see. Break your work into small, manageable tasks so you stay motivated throughout your work procedure. Get yourself organized. Unclutter your mind. Starve your distractions. Create that perfect environment so you can keep up with your work until you're done. Please choose to be successful and then stick to it.

You may feel like you're fatigued, or your mind will stop producing ideas and creativity after a while. But that's completely fine. Take a break. Set a timer for five minutes. Force yourself to work on the thing for five minutes, and after those five minutes, it won't feel too bad to keep going. Make a habit of doing the small tasks first, so they get out of the way, and you can harness your energy to tackle the more significant projects.

Reward yourself every time you complete your work. This will boost your confidence and will give you the strength to continue with your remaining tasks. Don't let your personal and professional responsibilities overwhelm you. Help yourself stay focused by keeping in mind that you're accountable for your own actions. Brian Roemmele, the Quora user, encourages people to own every moment, "You are in full control of this power. In your hands, you can build the tallest building and, in your hands, you can destroy the tallest buildings."

Start surrounding yourself with people who are an optimist and works hard. The saying goes, you're the average of the five people you hang out with the most. So, make sure you surround yourself with people who push you to succeed.

No matter how uninspired or de-motivating it may seem, you have to take that first step and start working. Whether it's a skill that you're learning, a language that you want to know, a dance step that you wish to perfect, a business idea that you want to implement, an instrument that you want to master, or simply doing the work for anyone else, you should do it immediately. Don't wait for the next minute, the next hour, the next day, or the following week; start doing your stuff. No one else is going to do your work for you, nor it's going to be completed by itself. Only you have the power to get on with it and get it done. Get your weak spots fixed. In the end, celebrate your achievements whether it's small or big. Imagine the relief of not having that task up on your plate anymore. Visualize yourself succeeding. It can help you stay to stay focused and motivated and get your work done. Even the worst tasks won't feel painful, but instead, they'll feel like a part of achieving something big.

Remember, motivation starts within. Find it, keep it and make it work wonders for you.

Chapter 20:

6 Ways On How To Make
Your Partner Feel Loved

The word partner has a deep meaning. It means the association with each other. They understand each other, respecting and supporting every step and decision of each other. In simple words, a partner indicates being fully committed to each other.

Being committed includes many challenges, but one of the biggest and the main challenges is how to make your partner feel loved. This is a big challenge because many partners still don't understand each other entirely after spending most of the time together. Efforts from both partners can help in this situation which can lead to a happy and healthy relationship.

Comforting each other in every situation, mostly in their challenging times, has always played a key role in making your partner feel loved. Your partner knows that you are always there to support them and expressing your willingness to make them relieved, and never doubt their decision.

1. Complementing Each Other

Many people think that the female partner in a relationship needs compliments, but the truth is every human being on this planet needs compliments sometimes. Compliments matter a lot, even for boys, but they don't show that they need compliments. Even if they are complimented, they don't show the happiness of being praised. Being praised by a stranger or not so close doesn't matter a lot, but if the compliment comes from an immediate or loved one, it means the world to them. Complimenting each other back and forth can also improve communication, which is the building block.

2. Be Attentive Towards Each Other

Taking each other for granted destroys a relationship. Instead, try to give all of your attention to your partner. It strengthens a connection. It makes them feel wanted. Listen to them with your complete attention. Listen to the first and then give your opinion or comfort them depending on the situation. Pay him the attention the partner deserves because every moment you spend with him is crucial. Whether planning a dinner or a movie night, always carve out time to be with each other. And when you're spending that quality time together, let things flow naturally and give your partner your undivided attention. Show your interest in them and make them feel that you want to be in their company.

3. Little Gestures of Love

Little gestures can also show your partner how much you care about them and make them feel special and loved. Small gestures can include checking on them, texting them, calling them to say how much you miss them, making plans to meet them, sending small meaningful gifts, asking how their day was and what they are doing tomorrow. Plan surprises for them. Randomly say how much you love them. These small gestures will make their day a hundred percent better.

4. Accept That

Acknowledge your partner. Appreciate them for what they are doing for you. Thank them for their attention and their support, and the love they have given. Thank them just for being there.No one is perfect. Everyone has flaws, and those flaws need to be accepted. A person can never be in front of the person they love until and unless the person they love accepts for who they are and accepts their flaws.

5. Appreciate Them

Make them feel special. Make them feel proud of who you have chosen as a partner. Tell them that it was the right decision to choose them as a partner. Send them appreciation paragraphs. Tell them that they are important and they matter and that you cannot take a step or decision without their opinion. Relive and remember your memories with them. Take a trip down memory lane once in a while. Cherish your happy memories, remember you are bad ones too, and promise each other that no more memories like these will ever be made again. Try not to break promises. Try to fulfill them.

6. Excite Each Other Up

Compliment his accomplishments. Tell him that you are proud of what he accomplished and how hard he worked for those accomplishments. Tell him how he deserved what he accomplished.

Conclusion:

Be abundant with happiness. Let your partner lead. Respect him. Be loyal and faithful and give your hundred percent. Be kind and forgive them. Never let your ego win, and never let pride enter your heart.

Chapter 21:

How To Be A Better Presenter

Have you ever wondered how the ted talker swept you off your feet by changing your visions and ideas in just A tiny amount of time? Or how they were so easy to make you believe in what they're selling, and now you're hanging on to every word they said, even if the time has passed? Or how charismatic and easy-going they seemed and won you over just like that? Let me reveal the answers to these questions. Well, you see, they were likable, concise, and persuasive; all the characteristics that we need to be great presenters, both on and off stage.

Drawing in your audience by having excellent presentation skills is an integral part of success. Whether you are leading A troop, being A founder of A company, A blogger who presents at events, or an employee who speaks to clients, you must be able to convey your ideas effectively and communicate excitement to your audience. Otherwise, how will you convince someone to buy into your vision, close that sale, or crush that job interview? It all comes down to being A better and persuasive presenter.

Public presenting is considered nothing short of A gift. You can speak in front of people every day, be it you being an author, an employee, or an entrepreneur; opportunities are given to you every day, and you should never squander them. Sure, there are A few things that you need to master to gain that confidence of presenting out loud, but once you're done, you will be able to see the changes. The first and foremost thing to do is master your core messages. It's stupid to think that not preparing your speech beforehand is okay, and you will be able to nail it the first time without even practicing. Practice makes perfect, and if you want to excel at anything, it comes with the condition to practice it A million times before you finally get it right. Practice your speech aloud with A recorder and then see for your mistakes. It's better to do this in private first and not wait for others to critique your speech for you.

Study and think about your audience. Your audience is your primary target. Make your presentations surrounding the ideas that your audience already knows and what they need to know further. The most critical part of any presentation is engaging your audience and trying to communicate effectively with them. An essential quality of being A presenter is that you should polish your confidence from time to time. Let go of any self-conscious concerns that you will have regarding your audience. The more you deliver confidently, the more the audience will give it back to you.

Master your introduction by getting right to the point. First impressions matter the most, so make sure you give them that right. The first words coming out of your mouth can either make or break your presentation, so make sure you say something that will grab their attention instantly.

Be relaxed! Put up A short story or an anecdotal joke in between to loosen the tension. Use open body language and supplemental facial expressions. Smile at them when appropriate but don't lose your sternness either. Learn how to locate your stress and keep eliminating it. Improving your presentation skills will help you in all aspects of your life; you will start having so many opportunities at your hand. You will see A massive increase in your success rate over time.

Chapter 22:

Deal With Your Fears Now

Fear is a strange thing.

Most of our fears are phantoms that never actually appear or become real,

Yet it holds such power over us that it stops us from making steps forward in our lives.

It is important to deal with fear as it not only holds you back but also keeps you caged in irrational limitations.

Your life is formed by what you think.

It is important not to dwell or worry about anything negative.

Don't sweat the small stuff, and it's all small stuff (Richard Carlson).

It's a good attitude to have when avoiding fear.

Fear can be used as a motivator for yourself.

If you're in your 30s, you will be in your 80s in 50 years, then it will be too late.

And that doesn't mean you will even have 50 years. Anything could happen.

But let's say you do, that's 50 years to make it and enjoy it.

But to enjoy it while you are still likely to be healthy, you have a maximum of 15 years to make it - minus sleep and living you are down to 3 years.

If however you are in your 40s, you better get a move on quickly.

Does that fear not dwarf any possible fears you may have about taking action now?

Dealing with other fears becomes easy when the ticking clock is staring you in the face.

Most other fears are often irrational.

We are only born with two fears, the fear of falling and the fear of load noises.

The rest have been forced on us by environment or made up in our own minds.

The biggest percentage of fear never actually happens.

To overcome fear we must stare it in the face and walk through it knowing our success is at the other side.

Fear is a dream killer and often stops people from even trying.

Whenever you feel fear and think of quitting, imagine behind you is the ultimate fear of the clock ticking away your life.

If you stop you lose and the clock is a bigger monster than any fear.

If you let anything stop you the clock will catch you.

So stop letting these small phantoms prevent you from living,

They are stealing your seconds, minutes, hours , days and weeks.

If you carry on being scared, they will take your months, years and decades.

Before you know it they have stolen your life.

You are stronger than fear but you must display true strength that fear will be scared.
It will retreat from your path forever if you move in force towards it because fear is fear and by definition is scared.

We as humans are the scariest monsters on planet Earth.
So we should have nothing to fear
Fear tries to stop us from doing our life's work and that is unacceptable.
We must view life's fears as the imposters they are, mere illusions in our mind trying to control us.

We are in control here.
We have the free will to do it anyway despite fear.
Take control and fear will wither and disappear as if it was never here.
The control was always yours you just let fear steer you off your path.

Fear of failure, fear of success, fear of what people will think.
All irrational illusions.
All that matters is what you believe.
If your belief and faith in yourself is strong , fear will be no match for your will.

Les Brown describes fear as false evidence appearing real.
I've never seen a description so accurate.

Whenever fear rears its ugly head, just say to yourself this is false evidence appearing real.

Overcoming fear takes courage and strength in one's self.
We must develop more persistence than the resistance we will face when pursuing our dreams.
If we do not develop a thick skin and unwavering persistence we will be beaten by fear, loss and pain.

Our why must be so important that these imposters become small in comparison.
Because after all the life we want to live does dwarf any fears or set back that might be on the path.
Fear is insignificant.
Fear is just one thing of many we must beat into the ground to prove our worth.
Just another test that we must pass to gain our success.

Because success isn't your right,
You must fight
With all your grit and might
Make it through the night and shine your massive light on the world.
And show everyone you are a star.

Chapter 23:

This Is Life

Who doesn't ponder the most basic and primary question, 'What is Life?' It is a bit cliche, but not unnecessary at all. And it certainly isn't illogical to think about what we are and what we have.

We often take life for granted but never realize what we have is special. We never contemplate the most important aspect of our existence.

We evolve during our time on this Earth. We start from nothing. But build towards a stronger being with greater and much better ambitions. We try to excel at everything we cross paths with. We strive towards our conscious development. We work towards our physical as well as emotional well-being.

We have a lot to live for but we rarely try to live for what matters the most. We never try to live like we have a greater purpose. Rather we try to go for petty things that might not even last for that long.

Life is short compared to what is going on around us. But we have to live it like there are unlimited seasons to come, each with its own blessings, each with its own opportunities.

We, humans, have evolved enough to be able to see beyond most plain things, but we chose to get soaked up in shallow waters. This life is a deep ocean with limits practically unpredictable.

Life is unexpected, it's unintentional, it's fussy but worth living for.

The life we see today is the collection of infinite, unbroken, and eternal events, rippling together simultaneously.

We say someone is alive when we see them breathing and moving but we never really know if that person is actually alive inside. We never really think about if the person is happy inside and enjoying what they have right now. We never try to look through the person and help them be alive for what matters.

Life never treats everyone the same way. But you don't need to get depressed every time you miss an alarm, or perform badly in an exam, or don't have the proper stats to show for your annual sales.

It doesn't always end badly and it certainly isn't bad every time of every day. It's just our psychology that makes us treat ourselves and life in a way that makes life demeaning and not worth it.

Everything is worth it once you try to look past the bad things and focus on the good ones you still get left with.

You have this one life, so go and live it like it matters the most to you. You might have to get a bit selfish and you might have to offend some people. Not deliberately, but just because you need some time and space which they might not allow, but it doesn't matter.

The epitome of life is that you have a clock ticking with each second getting you closer to the end. But you can still run around the clock and make it work as a swing. Enjoy with a purpose. Lead with your heart and you will come across wonders.

Chapter 24:

Becoming a Leader

Wow today we're going to talk about a topic that i think might not apply to everybody but it is one that is definitely interesting as well and good for everyone to know if they some day aspire to be a leader of sorts.

Leadership is something that does not come naturally to everyone, while some are born leaders as they say, in reality most of us requires life experiences, training, and simply good people skills in order to be an effective leader that is respected.

To be a respected leader, you have to have excellent communication skills who come across as fair and just to your employees while also being able to make tough decisions when the time comes.

I believe that leaders are not born, but their power is earned. A person who has not had the opportunities to deal with others on a social and business level can never be able to make effective decisions that serves the well being of others. A leader in any organisation is one that is able to command respect not by force but by implicit authority.

So what are some ways that you can acquire leadership skills if you feel that you lack experience in it? Well first of all i believe that putting yourself in more social and group settings in friendly situations is a good place to start. Instead of jumping right into a work project, you can start by organising an activity where you are in charge. For example those that involve team work and team games. Maybe an escape room, or even simply taking charge by organising a party and planning an event where you become the host, and that usually means that you are in charge of getting things in order and all the nitty gritty stuff. Planning parties, coordinating people, time management, giving instructions, preparing materials... All these little pieces require leadership to pull off. And with these practices in events that will not affect your professional career, after you get a good feel of what it is like, you can move on to taking on a leadership role in projects at school or work. And hopefully over time all these practices will add up and you will be a much more holistic leader.

Soft skills are a key part to being an effective leader as well. Apart from professional expertise at the work place. So i encourage you to be as proficient in your learning of people skills and mastering interpersonal communication as well as being fluent in all the intricacies and details of your job description.

If you require a higher level of leadership training, i would encourage you to sign up for a course that would put you in much more challenging situations where you will be put to the test. This may be the push that you need to get you on your path to be the leader that you always thought that you could be.

Personally, I have always been a leader, not of a team, but of my own path. That instead of following in the footsteps of someone, or taking orders from bosses, i like to take charge of what i do with my time. And how to manage my career in that fashion. As much as i would like to tell myself that i am an effective leader, more often that not, i can honestly say i wish i was better. I wish i was better at managing my time, at managing my finances, at managing my work, and I have to always upgrade my leadership skills to ensure that I am effective in what I do. That I do not waste precious time.

Your leadership goals might be different from mine. Maybe you have an aspiration to be a head of a company, or division, or to lead a group in charitable work, or to be a leader of a travel tour group. Being a leader comes in all forms and shapes, and your soft skills can definitely by transferable in all areas.

So i challenge you to take leadership seriously and to think of ways to improve your leadership skills by placing yourself in situations where you can fine tune every aspect of your personality when dealing with others. At the end of the day, how people perceive you may be the most important factor of all.

Chapter 25:

4 Ways to Deal with Feelings of Inferiority When Comparing to Others

When we're feeling inferior, it's usually a result of comparing ourselves to other people and feeling like we don't measure up. And let's be real, it happens all. The. Damn. Time. You could be scrolling through your Instagram feed, notice a new picture of someone you follow, and think: *Wow, how do they always look so perfect?! No amount of filters will make me look like that!* Or maybe you show up to a party, and you quickly realize you're in a room full of accomplished people with exciting lives, and the thought of introducing yourself sends you into a panic. Suddenly, you're glancing at the door and wondering what your best escape plan is. You could be meeting your partner's family for the first time, and you're worried that you won't fit in or that they'll think you're not good enough. You might feel easily intimidated by other people and constantly obsess over what they think of you, even though it's beyond your control.

Don't worry! We have some coping strategies for you that will help you work through your feelings. Try 'em out and see for yourself!

1. Engage in compassionate self-talk

When we feel inferior, we tend to pick ourselves apart and be hard on ourselves. Don't fall into the trap of being your own worst critic! Instead, build your self-confidence and self-esteem by saying positive things to yourself that resonate with you: *I'm feeling inferior right now, but I know my* worth. *I'm not defined by my credentials, my possessions, or my appearance. I am whole.*

2. Reach out for support or connect with a friend

Just like the Beatles song goes: *I get by with a little help from my friends!* Reach out to someone you can trust and who will be there for you. You might feel inferior now, but it doesn't mean you have to navigate it alone! Get all of those negative feelings off your chest. Having someone there to validate our feelings can be so helpful!

3. Give yourself a pep talk and utilize a helpful statement

Comparing ourselves to other people just brings down our mood and makes us feel like garbage. Sometimes, we gotta give ourselves a little pep talk to turn those negative thoughts around. *I feel inferior right now, but I can get through this! I'm not the only person who has felt this way, and I won't be the last. Everything is gonna be okay!*

4. Comfort yourself like a friend

If you don't have anyone who can be there for you at this moment, that's okay. You can be there for yourself! Think about how you would want a loved one to comfort you at this moment. Pat yourself on the back, treat yourself to some junk food, cuddle up on the couch with a warm, fuzzy blanket and binge your favorite show on Netflix. Be the friend you need right now!

Chapter 26:

Feeling That You Don't Have Enough Time

Today we're going to talk about a topic that I think many of us struggle with, myself included. The topic is about feeling that we don't have enough time to do the things that we need to do.

Personally I feel this one a daily basis, and it is partly because of my expectations versus reality. Many a times I set unrealistic expectations of how much time is required to do a particular task on my list that I tend to pack my schedule with way too many items. This leads me to feeling incredible overwhelm and stress because it just doesn't seem like I can get all my objectives down before 12am. We tend to underestimate the amount of time and energy that working on our goals require of us that many times we end up setting ourselves up for failure.

I would watch the clock go by minute by minute, hour by hour, only to find myself still working on the very first task on my list of 10 things to do. As you can already imagine I end up feeling that I'm not being productive, even though most of the time I am, and this feeling that I'm not doing things fast enough erodes my motivation further.

There are times when I am genuinely unproductive - like when I get lost in watching television, browsing the web, playing with my dog, being distracted for the sake of procrastination, and a myriad of reasons. But for the purposes of this topic, I will not be addressing those issues. I want to turn our attention to what we can actually accomplish if given enough time, assuming our level of productivity isnt affected by distractions.

The first thing we have to realise is that the things that we need to get done will take however long it needs to get done. Many times we may not be able to control or accurately measure the duration that a task may take. Instead of setting a time limit on a task, we should instead measure our productivity and be focused on doing rather than completing.

As an entrepreneur, I've come to learn that my work never ends. When I think I have finished one task, another one just comes crashing onto my desk like a meteor - another fire I have to put out, another problem I have to solve. I've come to realise that once I set a deadline for the time I need to complete something, rarely will I ever get it done on time. Most often I will be off by a long shot - either by the hours or even days.

Instead of setting arbitrary number of hours, I found that what worked best for me was to simply let my productivity flow. That I actually do more and accomplish more when I stop worrying about time itself - that I give my work however long it needs to get done and then call it a day.

This has allowed me to not be stressed that I never feel like I don't have enough time. Because in reality, time is relative. Time is something that I assign meaning to. If I simply focus on my designation, my 10 year plan, all I need to do is to simply work hard each day and that'll be good enough for me.

Right now the only thing that makes me feel like I don't have enough time, is when I actually waste them doing nothing meaningful. Having struggled with procrastination all my life, I've come to find out that I am not an innate workaholic. It doesn't come natural to me to want to do the work and that is what is causing me to feel like time is slipping away from me sometimes. That is something I have to continuously work on.

With regards to what you can learn from this - instead of racing against time to complete something, let the work flow out of you like water. Get into a state where productivity oozes out of you. Use a time tracking app to measure the amount of time that you have spent on working. Decide how much time you are willing to set aside to do your work and commit to that time. If 8 hours is the ideal, ensure that you clock those 8 hours and then end the day proud of yourself that you had already done what you set out to do at the start of the day. Never feel like you must do more and never beat yourself up for it. Be nicer to yourself as life is already hard enough as it is.

Another tip that I can recommend that has worked for me is to set a list of the top 3 things you want to do at the start of your day. Instead of the 10 that I did previously that caused me so much stress and anxiety, I have found that 3 is the ideal number of things that will bring us the most satisfaction and the least overwhelm when completing. If we are not able to complete those 3 big tasks, at least maybe we have done 1 or 2. We won't beat ourselves that we hadn't done those other 8 things at the back.

If on the other hand we have successfully completed all those 3 things by mid-day, we may choose to add another 3 items on our list. That way the carrot is never too far away and it is easily attainable should we want to add more.

So I challenge each and every one of you to look into your day with a new set of lens. Set your intentions right at the start of each day and focus on productivity on a focused set of 3 items. Let the work flow out of you and let the task complete its course naturally without rushing. Remember that it will take as long as it takes and you will only bring yourself more stress if you set a deadline on it. Use it only as a tool for motivation but nothing else if you must set a deadline. Don't be too hard on yourself. Focus on the journey and don't be overly stressed out by feeling that you're always racing against time.

Chapter 27:

It's All About Networking

Networking isn't merely the exchange of information with others — and it's certainly not about begging for favors. Networking is about establishing and nurturing long-term, mutually beneficial relationships with the people you meet, whether you're waiting to order your morning coffee, participating in an intramural sports league, or attending a work conference. You don't have to join several professional associations and attend every networking event that comes your way in order to be a successful networker. In fact, if you take your eyes off your smartphone when you're out in public, you'll see that networking opportunities are all around you every day.

Experts agree that the most connected people are often the most successful. When you invest in your relationships — professional and personal — it can pay you back in dividends throughout the course of your career. Networking will help you develop and improve your skill set, stay on top of the latest trends in your industry, keep a pulse on the job market, meet prospective mentors, partners, and clients, and gain access to the necessary resources that will foster your career development.

Career development, in its simplest terms, is the lifelong evolution of your career. It's influenced by a number of things that include the jobs you hold, the experiences you gain in and out of the office, the success you achieve at each stage of your career, the formal and informal education and training you receive, and the feedback you're provided with along the way.

Ideally, organizations would place more emphasis on employee development in the workplace. However, the reality is that we live in what Carter Cast, author of the book, "The Right (and Wrong) Stuff: How Brilliant Careers Are Made," refers to as "the era of do-it-yourself career development."

Cast explains that in today's workforce, the burden is on you to take control of your career development. Hence the importance of networking for career development: As you network with people at your company, in your industry, and even outside your field of interest, you'll uncover opportunities to connect with different types of mentors and advisors, increase your visibility with senior management, further develop your areas of expertise, and improve your soft skills. You may assume that networking is an activity reserved for your time out of the office and off the clock, but nothing could be further from the truth. While there is much value in connecting with people who work at other companies or in different fields, don't discount the importance of networking in the workplace. Whether you're new to the company and want to get the lay of the land or you're already established and have your sights set on a promotion, networking with your co-workers can be incredibly beneficial to your career progression.

As you develop relationships with those in your department and in other divisions, be on the lookout for potential mentors, upcoming professional development opportunities, or new job opportunities that are not publicly advertised. It's never too early — or too late — to invest in your network. The best way to improve your networking skills is to put yourself out there and give it a try. According to Baikowitz, "the worst networking mistake you can make is not trying at all."

Chapter 28:

How To Find Motivation

Today we're going to talk about a topic that hopefully will help you find the strength and energy to do the work that you've told yourself you've wanted or needed to but always struggle to find the one thing that enables you to get started and keep going. We are going to help you find motivation.

In this video, I am going to break down the type of tasks that require motivation into 2 distinct categories. Health and fitness, and work. As I believe that these are the areas where most of you struggle to stay motivated. With regards to family, relationships, and other areas, i dont think motivation is a real problem there.

For all of you who are struggling to motivate yourself to do things you've been putting off, for example getting fit, going to the gym, motivation to stay on a diet, to keep working hard on that project, to study for your exams, to do the chores, or to keep working on your dreams... All these difficult things require a huge amount of energy from us day in and day out to be consistent and to do the work.

I know... it can be incredibly difficult. Having experienced these ups and downs in my own struggle with motivation, it always starts off swimmingly... When we set a new year's resolution, it is always easy to think that we will stick to our goal in the beginning. We are super motivated to go do the gym to lose those pounds, and we go every single day for about a week... only to give up shortly after because we either don't see results, or we just find it too difficult to keep up with the regime.

Same goes for starting a new diet... We commit to doing these things for about a week, but realize that we just simply don't like the process and we give up as well...

Finding motivation to study for an important exam or working hard on work projects are a different kind of animal. As these are things that have a deadline. A sense of urgency that if we do not achieve our desired result, we might fail or get fired from our company. With these types of tasks, most of us are driven by fear, and fear becomes our motivator... which is also not healthy for us as stress hormones builds within us as we operate that way, and we our health pays for it.

Let's start with tackling the first set of tasks that requires motivation. And i would classify this at the health and fitness level. Dieting, exercise, going to the gym, eating healthily, paying attention to your sleep... All these things are very important, but not necessarily urgent to many of us. The deadline we set for ourselves to achieve these health goals are arbitrary. Based on the images we see of models, or people who seem pretty fit around us, we set an unrealistic deadline for ourselves to achieve those body goals. But more often than not, body changes don't happen in days or weeks for most of us by the way we train. It could take up to months or years... For those celebrities and fitness models you see on Instagram or movies, they train almost all day by personal trainers. And their deadline is to look good by the start of shooting for the movie. For most of us who have day jobs, or don't train as hard, it is unrealistic to expect we can achieve that body in the same amount of time. If we only set aside 1 hour a day to exercise, while we may get gradually fitter, we shouldn't expect that amazing transformation to happen so quickly. It is why so many of us set ourselves up for failure.

To truly be motivated to keep to your health and fitness goals, we need to first define the reasons WHY we even want to achieve these results in the first place. Is it to prove to yourself that you have discipline? Is it to look good for your wedding photoshoot? Is it for long term health and fitness? Is it so that you don't end up like your relatives who passed too soon because of their poor health choices? Is it to make yourself more attractive so that you can find a man or woman in your life? Or is it just so that you can live a long and healthy life, free of medical complications that plague most seniors by the time they hit their 60s and 70s? What are YOUR reasons WHY you want to keep fit? Only after you know these reasons, will you be able to truly set a realistic deadline for your health goals. For those that are in it for a better health overall until their ripe old age, you will realize that this health goal is a life long thing. That you need to treat it as a journey that will take years and decades. And small changes each day will add up. Your motivator is not to go to the gym 10 hours a day for a week, but to eat healthily consistently and exercise regularly every single day so that you will still look and feel good 10, 20, 30, 50 years, down the road.

And for those that need an additional boost to motivate you to keep the course, I want you to find an accountability partner. A friend that will keep you in check. And hopefully a friend that also has the same health and fitness goals as you do. Having this person will help remind you not to let yourself and this person down. Their presence will hopefully motivate you to not let your guard down, and their honesty in pointing out that you've been slacking will keep you in check constantly that you will do as you say.

And if you still require an additional boost on top of that, I suggest you print and paste a photo of the body that you want to achieve and the idol that you wish to emulate in terms of having a good health and fitness on a board where you can see every single day. And write down your reasons why beside it. That way, you will be motivated everytime you walk past this board to keep to your goals always.

Now lets move on to study and work related tasks. For those with a fixed 9-5 job and deadlines for projects and school related work, your primary motivator right now is fear. Which as we established earlier, is not exactly healthy. What we want to do now is to change these into more positive motivators. Instead of thinking of the consequences of not doing the task, think of the rewards you would get if you completed it early. Think of the relief you will feel knowing that you had not put off the work until the last minute. And think of the benefits that you will gain... less stress, more time for play, more time with your family, less worry that you have to cram all the work at the last possible minute, and think of the good results you will get, the opportunities that you will have seized, not feeling guilty about procrastinations... and any other good stuff that you can think of. You could also reward yourself with a treat or two for completing the task early. For example buying your favourite food, dessert, or even gadgets. All these will be positive motivators that will help you get the ball moving quicker so that you can get to those rewards sooner. Because who likes to wait to have fun anyway?

Now I will move on to talk to those who maybe do not have a deadline set by a boss or teacher, but have decided to embark on a new journey by themselves. Whether it be starting a new business, getting your accounting done, starting a new part time venture.. For many of these tasks, the only motivator is yourself. There is no one breathing down your neck to get the job done fast and that could be a problem in itself. What should we do in that situation? I believe with this, it is similar to how we motivate ourselves in the heath and fitness goals. You see, sheer force doesn't always work sometimes. We need to establish the reasons why we want to get all these things done early in life. Would it be to fulfil a dream that we always had since we were a kid? Would it be to earn an extra side income to travel the world? Would it be to prove to yourself that you can have multiple streams of income? Would it to become an accomplished professional in a new field? Only you can define your reasons WHY you want to even begin and stay on this new path in the first place. So only you can determine why and how you can stay on the course to eventually achieve it in the end.

Similarly for those of you who need additional help, I would highly recommend you to get an accountability partner. Find someone who is in similar shoes as you are, whether you are an entrepreneur, or self-employed, or freelance, find someone who can keep you in check, who knows exactly what you are going through, and you can be each other's pillars of support when one of you finds yourself down and out. Or needs a little pick me up. There is a strong motivator there for you to keep you on course during the rough time.

And similar to health and fitness goal, find an image on the web that resonates with the goal you are trying to achieve. Whether it might be to buy a new house, or to become successful, i want that image to always be available to you to look at every single day. That you never forget WHY you began the journey. This constant reminder should light a fire in you each and everyday to get you out of your mental block and to motivate you to take action consistently every single day.

So I challenge each and every one of you to find motivation in your own unique way. Every one of you have a different story to tell, are on different paths, and no two motivators for a person are the same. Go find that one thing that would ignite a fire on your bottom every time you look at it. Never forget the dream and keep staying the course until you reach the summit.

Chapter 29:

<u>10 Habits of Warren Buffet</u>

Warren Buffett, popularly known as the "Oracle of Omaha", is the chairman and CEO of Berkshire Hathaway and an American investor, corporate magnate, and philanthropist. He's undoubtedly a well-known investor of all time-if, not history, continuously setting records of knowledge, talent, and a strong drive to reach his future objectives. Buffett is also a supporter of leadership and personal growth, and he shares his wealth of advice to help you better your decisions.

So, how did he land to success? Here are ten warren's habits, which would you benefits later on.

1. His Reading Habit

Reading- a habit that he adheres to religiously, is one rule that Warren Buffett considers key to success. So he reads The Wall Street Journal, USA Today, and Forbes in the mornings and The Financial Times, The New York Times, Omaha World-Herald, and American Banker throughout the day.

Reading is basic to improving your understanding. Among other books, self-improvement books are popular with Buffet. That's said, consider jogging your memory with a mind-stimulating activity like reading. Engage in "500" pages book, article, newspaper each day, in the area that self-improves your interests. Reading makes you more knowledgeable than other people.

2. Compound Your Life and Finances

As per Albert Einstein, "Compound interest is the world's eighth wonder." if you understand it, you earn it; if not, you pay it." Warren Buffet's approach to investments never changes. He maintains his compounding investment principle as an investing strategy and aligns it with thinking patterns.

Compounding is the practice of reinvesting your earnings in your principal to generate an exponential return. Are you compounding your life finances, relationships, reading? That is how knowledge operates. It accumulates in the same way that compound interest does. You can accomplish it, but best when you're determined!

3. Isolation Power

Despite becoming the world's best investor and stock market trader, Warren Buffett claims that living away from Wall Street helped him. When you block the outside influence, you think quickly, distract unimportant variables and the general din.

Isolation exposes you to more prospects as it keeps you from external influence and information, making you unique and infamous.

4. Managing Your Time Wisely

You'll have 24 hours a day, or 1,440 minutes. All the leaders and successful people like Warren have one thing in common because of how powerful it is: Time management.

5. Do What You Enjoy

Your career or business may start with low returns but approaching it in Warren's way means switching your mind entirely to the job. If your mind likes something and you feed it to it regularly, it never turns off.

Working for a low salary is a momentary inconvenience, but it multiplies at the rate your skills increases, and they grow tremendously because you enjoy doing it.

6. Inner and Outer Scorecards

The key question about how people act is whether they have an Internal or an outward scorecard. So, naturally, it is preferable to be happy with your Inner Score to live a peaceful and happy life.

Having an inner scorecard is being contented with your thoughts and making decisions based on those thoughts while ignoring external influences or judgement skills. The deal is to live through values that matter to you, especially when making tough financial decisions.

7. Mimic the Finest Managers' Leadership Behaviours

Much of your life endeavours are, in most cases, shaped by the person who you choose to admire and emulate. Warren's admiration of Tom Murphy scourged him to greatness in leading his businesses to success.

8. Understand What You Have

Know and understand the companies in which you have a stake. Examine and analyze what is going on within the company, not what is going on in the marketplace.

The company's operations should be straightforward such that you can explain to an 8-year-old child how the company produces money in one phase. Familiarize enough with your investments while keeping a tab with its exact worth.

9. Invest in Your Well-Being

The basic right towards success is your well-being. Take care of your mental and physical health first, especially when you're young. The importance of life's fundamentals- nutritious diet, regular exercise, and restful sleep-is self-evident. It all boils down to whether you're doing them correctly.

10. Create a Positive Reputation

Buffett's reputation stems from his moral and level-headed attitude to both his personal and business life. You should view your business/career as a reflection of yourself, which means you should be careful and sensitive of how your decisions influence others.

Conclusion

Just as Warren, enhance your cognitive skills through learning to become more knowledgeable for bettering your life initiatives. While focusing on your major goals, take care of your mental and physical well-being. Therefore, invest your efforts and time carefully because the returns will multiply eventually.

Chapter 30:

Building Confidence

The things we strive for all our lives are a mere image of what we can achieve and what we want to achieve.

There is a difference between two very important aspects of our life. One is self-esteem and the other is self-confidence. You have very high self-esteem if you think big of yourself and have respect for your craft. This is a very important thing to have because no one is big on confidence if they don't have a good opinion about themselves.

We often say that 'You and You only are your best critic'. This isn't a statement for the narrow-minded.

If you think big of yourself, you will have a better perspective of the things you do and wish to do someday. If you have a 'No Go' confidence towards everything, then you have nothing to start with.

Do you want to build confidence? Take some tips, just as a piece of advice.

If you want to build confidence, Focus on what you can't do, not on what you can't. I know this is against everything we think someone will say to boost your morale.

But the truth is, that when you start to work on things that you cannot do, you will try it for some time, but then you will eventually fail. That might prove to be a breaking point for some people.

If you focus on what you can do, you will always be successful. And you will praise your good work, and that will help you every time exponentially. The more you proceed, the more you will succeed and the more you will be confident in yourself.

You also need to surround yourself with people who believe in you.

Every person in his life has had a moment when they were just about to summit the biggest achievement of their life. But gave up or lost hope because they let the noise and opinions around them get into their heads.

Those who have opinions have nothing else going on in their lives. So they try to mend their souls by inflicting negation on others. You don't have time or energy to deal with these people.

So keep the people in your life who have the same approach towards life as you and they love you for who you are. These people will help you in even the darkest deepest days of your life.

The last piece of advice is what we have heard from the first step that we took in our childhood. The advice of never giving up!

You will fail here and there everywhere in your life. You are meant to fail. Everyone is meant to fail someday. But you cannot give up! You Should Never Give Up!

We have a lot of things going on in our lives and one or the other is meant to fall apart someday. We lose money. We lose friends. We lose family. But what you cannot lose forever is Hope.

Till the day you have hope, you have a reserve to keep you on the track and maybe someday, fly like a phoenix.

Chapter 31:

How To Stick To Your Goals When Life Gets Crazy

Life Can Be Rocky

We all can agree that life can sometimes be noisy and messy. It can be chaos and madness and a single voice of reason in a room may lack. When life gets crazy, priorities change, and goalposts are sometimes shifted in the heat of the moment. Life is indiscriminate of your age or gender and it can turn your goals upside down.

Sanity vanishes in thin air when life is marred by confusion. In this state, you will most likely replace your goals with others because they look more relevant and probably easily attainable.

Many people abandon 'fragile' goals when life gets bumpy. Some argue that a mouth-to-hand lifestyle is not ideal when chasing after your goals. Do not get mixed up in this confusion, retreat to sobriety and ask yourself whether you will do the blame game or work towards your goals. Be assertive with yoursrightelf.

Get Your Priorities

Define your goals and how you intend to follow up on each one to completion. You cannot stick to vague goals. They have to be clear in your mind and the route to chase after them should be outlined awaiting execution. The common mistake most people commit is to say they will cross the bridge when they get there. This form of procrastination is misleading. Live the present and plan for the future.

A good plan is a job half done. Nothing should steal your focus from knowing your priorities. Not even the craze of life. Prioritize what is important and snob anything outside the plan no matter how lucrative or tempting it may present itself.

Have Well-Founded Goals

The foundation of your goals matters the most in determining whether you will stick to them or not. Some people set unrealistic goals because of external influence and peer pressure. If you fall within this category, you will be chasing after an illusion and living a lie because your dreams are not in tandem with your personality.

Well-founded goals go beyond convenience. You set them based on your ability and vision of how you want to live your life. It should be devoid of exaggeration and imitation of the lifestyles of celebrities. You will be able to stick to your goals if you are true to yourself.

Authenticity and fidelity to the kind of person you are will glue you to your goals. Is not that the dream you want to live?

Superfluous goals are changed from time to time for convenience. Question your commitment to your goals when you start shifting goalposts.

Have A Thorough Understanding Of Your Environment

We are products of our environments. The role your environment plays in your life cannot be ignored. A toxic and unfriendly environment is incapable of manifesting your good goals. Instead, it will poison you to turn your back on the goals you had set. You may be a good person with pure intentions but your environment waters down all the gains you could achieve.

It is beneficial to exist in a good environment. It will channel positive energy your way to incubate your goals to their manifestation. Take time to understand your work or home environment and alienate yourself from any negative influence. It is better to be safe than sorry.

If circumstances demand, you can change your residence just to have a clear head to enable you to stick to your goals. Embrace positivity and watch yourself grow into the person you intend to be.

Audit Your List of Friends

Have you ever heard of the saying that you are the average of your five friends? The impact of your friends on your life cannot be underscored. They, in cahoots with your environment, have the potential to ensure whether or not you stick to and realize your goals.

Sit down to rethink the type of people you consider to be your friends. If they are wayward, they will pull you away from your goals. They will want you to be like them and possibly make you abandon your goals if they do not align with theirs.

Your success in sticking to your goals even when life gets crazy is pegged on your choice of associates. Choose them carefully.

Consume Inspirational and Motivational Content

Sometimes we need some positive energy in our lives to lift our spirits and soothe us that everything will be alright. Following your goals is a bumpy ride if there is nobody to encourage you. Read, listen and watch success stories to be encouraged.

Sticking to your goals is a conscious decision one makes and works towards it daily. You need a voice of reason to rise above that of discouragement. Finally, reason prevails and you get encouraged even when at the brink of giving up.

In conclusion, it has become the norm for life to get crazy. Responsibilities bombard us right, left, and center. You need to be inseparable from your goals for you to achieve them.

Chapter 32:

How To Spend Money Wisely.

Financial struggles could be of many types, I.E., Not bringing in enough money, not spending money wisely, or simply spending more money than making. According to time, nearly 73% of Americans die in debt. Sure, we're guilty of slipping up at one point or the other. It's quite easy to fall into the habit of buying expensive coffee every day, eating out or ordering takeaways, and getting our hands on groceries that we have eventually ended up throwing out. We don't have to be an expert in personal finances nor have A big investment portfolio to be financially secure. It is, however, essential to understand the basics of financial planning.

Before you can start figuring out how to spend your money wisely, you need to analyse and understand where exactly your money is going. Make A budget to track both your expenses and your income. Once you get your hands on where the money is going, you can start looking for better opportunities where they could be spent instead.

Need I tell you that far too many purchases are impulse decisions? It can be fine on A shorter scale, like buying A $1 chocolate, but it can become A serious problem for larger purchases. Before you buy something, think about A few factors first; like how it's going to affect you in the future, how long is it going to last, is it going to put you in debt, is the value you will get out of it over its lifetime worth the cost. These are the questions that you really should ask yourself to determine if the product is worth buying or are you only satisfying your inner cravings.

The average person spends far too much money in trying to maintain an image in front of others. Fancy cars, brand-name clothing, expensive watches, and perfumes, all these that we buy have more to do with impressing others than it does with purchasing something that we want to enjoy. This pursuit is far too expensive and unnecessary. Buy the things that you enjoy yourself and never fall prey to the feeling that you have to spend your money in bulk to impress people.

After you have started to track your finances, you can keep an eye on the habits that may be draining your budget. These habits could include expensive hobbies, eating out too much, stress shopping, spending loads of money on your friends/partner, or any number of other financial drains. Once you have figured out which habits are eating up large portions of your income, you can then self-evaluate whether these habits are actually worth your money or not.

Some people are naturally good at saving money. They draw enjoyment from growing their wealth. While for others, money is something that is spent the moment it reaches their hands. Anything else feels like A wasted opportunity for them. If you find yourself falling in the latter category, try and adopt A mentality that values savings over products. In the end, money spent on products that will wear or become uninteresting will always be lesser than money invested or money saved that will always benefit you.

Spending your money wisely isn't always about just avoiding unnecessary purchases - it also requires you to take the money that you save and put it towards your financial goals. With that in mind, it's never going to be about starting investing too early or too late. No matter how young or old you are, invest your money in things that will benefit you. Your spent money growing in value as time goes on is always A wise use of it.

Chapter 33:

9 Habits To Wake Up Early

Waking up early is a real struggle for many people. People are battling this friendly monster silently. Friendly because the temptation to snooze the alarm or turn it off completely when it rings in the morning is irresistible. Almost everyone can attest to cursing under their breath when they hear their alarm go off loudly in the morning.

Here are 9 habits that you should strive to incorporate into your life if you wish to make waking early a part of your routine:

1. Sleeping early.

It is simple – early to bed, early to rise. Retiring to bed early will give you enough time to exhaust your sleep. The average person ought to have at least 8 hours of sleep. Sleeping early will create more time for rest and enable you to wake up on time.

Since sleep is not ignorable, you may be embarrassed when you find yourself sleeping when attending a meeting, or when you are at work. Save yourself this shame by sleeping early to wake up earlier.

After a long day of vicissitudes, gift your body the pleasure of having a good night's rest. Create extra time for this by lying horizontally early enough.

2.   Scheduling your plans for the day beforehand.

A good plan is a job half done. Before the day ends, plan for the activities of the next day. When it is all mapped out, you will sleep with a clear mind on what you will be facing the next day. Planning is not a managerial routine task alone but everyone's duty of preparing to fight the unknown the following day.

Waking up early is a difficult decision to make impromptu because of the weakness in yielding to the temptation of 'sleeping for only five more minutes.' Having a plan gives you a reason to wake up early.

3.   Creating deadlines.

Working under pressure is an alternative motivation for waking up early if planning has failed. With assignments to submit within a short time, or work reports to be submitted on short notice, the need to wake up early to beat these deadlines will be automatic.

We can create deadlines and ultimatums for ourselves without waiting on our superiors to impose them on us. This self-drive will last longer and it will increase our productivity instead of waiting for our clients and employers to give us ultimatums.

4.   Being psychologically prepared.

The mind is the powerhouse of the body. Mental preparedness is the first step towards making and sticking to landmark decisions. The mind should initiate and accept the idea of waking up early before you can comfortably adopt this new routine.

Develop a positive attitude towards rising early and all other subsequent results will fall in place. The first person you need to convince to move towards a particular cause is you. As simple as waking up early seems, many people are grappling with late coming.

This is fixable by making a conscious decision to turn around your sleeping habits. The greatest battle is fought in the mind, where the body antagonizes the spirit.

5. <u>Finding like-minded friends.</u>

Birds of the same feathers flock together. When you are in the company of friends with one routine, your habits are fortified. With no dissenting voice amongst your friends to discourage you from waking up early, your morning routine will find a permanent spot in your life.

The contrary is true. When you are the odd one out in a clique of friends who have no regard for time, you are likely to lose even the little time-consciousness you had. They will contaminate you with their habits and before you know it, you will slip back to your old self (an over sleeper).

When you also decide to be a loner and not associate with those with the same habits as yourself, then you risk giving up on the way. The psych from friends will be lacking and soon you will just revert to your old habits.

When you want to walk fast, walk alone. When you want to go far, walk with others.

6. Being sensitive to your environment.

It takes a man of understanding to read and understand the prevailing times and seasons. You may occasionally visit a friend or a relative and spend the night. How can you wake up way past sunrise in a foreign environment? This will suggest to your hosts that you are lazy.

Create a good image by waking up a little bit early. If allowed, help do some morning chores over there.

Adjust your routine accordingly. Win over people by waking up early to join them in their morning chores. It is there where friendships are forged. A simple habit of waking up early can be an avenue to make alliances.

7. Addressing any health issues early.

In case of any underlying health conditions that can stop you from waking up early in the morning, seek medical help fast. You may be willing to be an early riser but may be suffering from asthma triggered by the chilly weather in the morning.

When that condition is controlled, you can also manage to wake up a little bit earlier than before and engage in health-friendly activities in the morning. It is a win-win. In either case, going for a medical check-up frequently will keep you healthy to wake up early.

Your health is a priority and when taken care of you will wake up early.

8. It is a habit for the successful.

Ironically, those who have made it in life wake up earlier than the less established ones. One would think that it is the place of the less-founded ones to rise early to go to work and do business so that they can be at par with the wealthy and mighty. Instead, the reverse is true.

Follow the footsteps of great leaders who wake up early to attend to their affairs. They have become who they are because they give no room to the laziness of waking up late. We all have 24 hours in a day to do our businesses, where does the gap between the haves and the have-nots come from? That gap comes from how we use our time.

9. Having a cheerful Spirit.

A cheerful spirit finds joy in even what seems trivial. You should not see waking up early as punishment. It should be a routine to be followed happily religiously. When you have a cheerful spirit, knowing for whose benefit you rise early, then it will be a habit engraved into your spirit.

The above 9 habits to wake up early are key to discovering our purpose and build a new routine henceforth of being an early riser. The most successful people in the world abide by this routine so why not make it yours too.

Chapter 34:

Do The Painful Things First

There are a lot of secret recipes to be happier; one of them is; seek what's painful first. Sure, this may sound a little ironic, but you will be surprised to know that all scientific research is behind this. Behavioural scientists discovered that one of the most effective ways to create an enjoyable experience is to stack the painful parts of the experience early in the process. For example, if you're a doctor, a lawyer, accountant, etc., it's better to break bad news first and then finish with the good news. This will give the clients a more satisfying experience since you start poorly then end on a solid note instead of starting well and ending badly.

There's a couple of crucial reasons why we should do the painful things first. We know that we have limited willpower during the day, and we also know that the most painful activities or tasks are sometimes the most difficult ones. So if we complete the things we find the most difficult first, we'll be exerting less energy on less complicated activities for the rest of the day. Scientific studies show that our prefrontal cortex (creative part of the brain) is the most active the moment we wake up. At the same time, the analytical parts of our brain (the editing and proofreading parts) become more active as the day goes on.

Another reason to do the painful activities first-hand after you wake up is that you would be freed from all the distractions and tend to do these tasks more quickly. If you delay the complex tasks, it will only come back to bite you. Starting with only one task for a day can be enough, as it could lead you to achieve more of them as time goes by. Things like building a new business, losing weight, or learning a new skill require pain and slow work in the beginning to get momentum. But after some persistence, you will likely see your improvements. Behavioral psychology suggests that we're more likely to lead a happier life if we're making improvements over time. Anthony Robbins once said, "If you're not growing, you're dying."

Making slow but gradual improvements is where persistency comes in. It's going to be painful and frustrating initially, and you won't learn a new language in an instant, or your business won't thrive immediately. But when you decide to sacrifice your short-term pleasure for a future pay-off, you will get to enjoy the long-term benefits over a sustained period. Stop avoiding what's hard; embrace it for your long-term happiness.

CPSIA information can be obtained
at www.ICGtesting.com
Printed in the USA
LVHW051125010222
709871LV00016B/2506